D0050646

The
Education of a
Very Young Madam

Ma-Ling Lee

with Christa Bourg

SCRIBNER

New York   London   Toronto   Sydney

SCRIBNER
A Division of Simon & Schuster, Inc.
1230 Avenue of the Americas
New York, NY 10020

The events and people in this book are real. Only the names, including the author's, and some of the details have been changed.

First Scribner Hardcover edition January 2009

SCRIBNER and design are trademarks of The Gale Group, Inc., used under license by Simon & Schuster, Inc., the publisher of this work.

For information about special discounts for bulk purchases, please contact Simon & Schuster Special Sales at 1-800-456-6798 or business@simonandschuster.com.

DESIGNED BY ERICH HOBBING

Text set in Granjon

Manufactured in the United States of America

1   3   5   7   9   10   8   6   4   2

Library of Congress Control Number: 2008026342

ISBN-13: 978-0-7432-8975-7
ISBN-10: 0-7432-8975-7

To "Zoe"

I've said there is no loyalty in money but you are the one exception.
Through all the trials and tribulations,
I found the most exceptional soul in you and will love,
appreciate, and cherish you forever.
You are my best friend, my only family,
and the most beautiful person I have ever encountered.
No matter what life has in store for us,
just know that you will forever remain in my heart.

Contents

The
Education of a
Very Young Madam

Prologue

It was summertime and I wanted to get out of New Jersey. A circuit seemed like the perfect way to do it. I'd thought about starting my own circuit for a long time, a sort of traveling ho show where I'd set up business in a city temporarily, advertise a few places, build up a local client list, and then move on to the next location before things got too hot. I'd never tried it before because it's too much work to handle on my own, but with my friend and new partner, Zoe, along to help book appointments and take most of the calls, I knew we could pull it off. And we did. We traveled all over the country, sometimes just the two of us, sometimes with another girl or even two or three meeting us in places like D.C., New York, Pennsylvania, Virginia, and Boston. And we made some serious cash that summer.

It was in Boston where my luck took a bad turn. Zoe and I had been riding high and managed to save more than $20,000 in cash, and that's after we went on a serious shopping spree. Newbury Street in Boston is one of my favorite places to shop in the whole world, and I have a serious designer shoe habit. Zoe, on the other hand, was not only a cheap and clueless ho when she started working for me, she dressed like one too. I had been slowly teaching her the difference between Prada and Payless, and the clients were beginning to notice the change.

We stayed in one upscale hotel while Zoe worked out of another one nearby. At the end of the week, however, I told Zoe to just use our room for her appointments since I wasn't going to be there. I planned to drive to New York to spend the weekend with a guy I had just started seeing. Scorpio, as he called himself, was a dancer—my favorite type of man—and I was really into him. Fully expecting to return a couple of days later, I packed up only a few clothes to bring with me. I left the rest of my belongings, including my computer, our stash of cash, and even my gun, behind with Zoe.

I got into New York Friday night and had a great time with Scorpio. On Saturday morning I woke up late and called Zoe's room just to check on her. A man answered the phone.

"Who's this?" I demanded, figuring Zoe had booked an early client who was cheeky enough to answer the phone. Either that or she'd gone out the night before with some friends and met someone.

"This is Officer Dan of the Boston Police Department. Who's this?" the man demanded right back.

I hung up the phone and freaked out.

CHAPTER 1

A Very Young Madam

Now's probably the time to tell you, I'm a madam. I run an upscale escort agency that caters to professional clientele in suburban New Jersey. In fact, by most small business standards, I've been *very* successful. With up to ten girls working for me at a time, my agency generates up to $40,000 in income each week, mostly in cash.

When people ask, I tell them I'm in the service industry or in marketing, and that's really pretty close to the truth. Girlfriend Experience (GFE for short), which is one of the names my agency goes by, is about more than just sex. It's about customer satisfaction, about creating a pleasurable experience for our clients.

We are no wham-bam-thank-you-ma'am kind of organization. My girls treat clients as if they are on the best date of their lives. They use videos and mood lighting, they wear lingerie, they ask about your fantasies. In the employee handbook that I give to all of my "entertainers," I offer a dozen different suggestions on ways they can personalize each encounter. That's right, we have an employee handbook, just like any other business, which should indicate to you that I am serious about the way I do things. It lays out what my girls are responsible for (paying for their own travel arrangements, being on time for appointments) and what's expected of them (treating customers with respect, cleaning up their hotel rooms before the next client arrives). It also offers some hints and tips about how to deliver truly exceptional service, from what to wear, to what kinds of background music are appropriate, to how to create a seductive atmosphere that will please any client.

Of course, what we're offering is a sure-thing date, which adds to the appeal. But my "sure things" are not always as sure as you might think. I book all the appointments, but every one of my girls has absolute veto power. If someone shows up at the door and turns a girl off in any way, for any reason—she gets a bad vibe or the guy scares her or he's too old or too drunk or even too black (I have one girl who is half black herself but will only do white guys . . . go figure)—then I let her off the hook without any questions. It's her life and her body, and she should be able to say no whenever she wants to.

When that kind of thing happens, I have to scramble to make the rejected guy feel better. We're a customer-service-oriented organization after all. I've found that the best thing to do in situations like these is to humble myself. I call the guy up and say, "I'm so sorry, honey, the girl just has some issues," which is not too hard to believe since most girls in this business have some issues. Then I say, "I should have known better. Let me make it up to you. Your next appointment is on me." (Or possibly just half price, depending on how mad he is.)

That always works. I've never had a guy say no to a freebie.

Girls in this business come in all sorts—different races, ages, economic backgrounds, religious affiliations, even education levels. Some are married; some aren't. Some have kids; some don't. Some have been married multiple times and have kids with multiple guys. They do this work for all sorts of reasons too—for money, for drugs, to get back at someone in their lives, to assert their independence, because they like it, because they don't like themselves—but one thing they seem to have in common is that they are all a little (or sometimes a lot) fucked up in the head.

One of my girls, for example, got stuck in Manhattan once and was looking for a way back to New Jersey. My driver was in the city and I didn't need him, so I called her up and said, "Why don't you just go back with my assistant?" She was really appreciative on the phone, but the next time I talked to her, she was furious with me.

"Why would you recommend that guy to me?" she screamed. "He was such a lousy lay. It was one of the worst nights of my life!"

"You slept with him?" I asked her. I was stunned. He was only nineteen, a reliable driver but kind of a tool, so I didn't understand why she'd do that.

"Of course I did. You told me to."

"I was only suggesting you get a ride with the guy, not that you actually *ride* him!" I said. "What were you thinking?"

"Oh," she replied, much more calmly now, "that makes more sense. I couldn't understand why you'd give me such bad advice about something like that. I thought maybe you were mad at me."

Who else but a ho would think I was offering her anything other than transportation? The girls I work with are even more likely to be nuts than your average hooker because I hire only professionals, which means they've been doing this for a while—no first-timers or girls who just want to see what it's like. Maybe it's not their exclusive profession—I've had housewives, students, artists . . . lots of women who do it only part-time—but none of the women who work for me are new to this. If they were, I wouldn't hire them, because I want only girls who know how to give good service.

A business like mine that offers high-end service didn't even exist in this corner of the world until I got here. When I first came to New Jersey, the highest price anyone paid for a girl was around $175 an hour. Nobody charged anything close to what I do now—typically $300 to $350 for an hour or less—because they never would have gotten away with it. The agencies were all using untrained girls and booking them into seedy motels in bad neighborhoods. It wasn't that hard for me to get customers when I moved here, especially the kinds of regular, stable, upscale customers I wanted.

There is plenty of money in New Jersey, so that was never the problem. I can only assume that the kind of agency I run didn't exist then because no one knew how to run one. (Of course, now that I've had a successful agency for several years, copycats have begun to pop up all over the place.) I did very simple things to distinguish myself, like hire professionals who are experienced and know how to give quality care. I use only three-star or higher hotels, which, ironically, are often cheaper than those seedy motels when booked through discount Internet sites. It wasn't brain surgery, but still, customer service, discretion, and reliability are all qualities that can be difficult to come by in this business, and clients appreciate them. They also happily pay more for them. In fact, if you devalue your girls by offering discounted rates, it can take some of the thrill out of the whole experience for the client (not to mention the fact that girls, just like employees of any kind of business, won't work as hard if they're being paid subpar wages). A guy wants to feel like he's paying for something special, and, obviously, lessening the thrill is the last thing I want to do.

Price points are always a balancing act, and it's certainly possible to charge too much as well. Right across the water from us in New York City, there are a number of agencies that regularly charge $1,500 an hour or more. I've done my homework on the subject and have basically come to the realization that, as alluring as they may be for both the entertainer and the agency, prices like that are just a mistake.

Let's face it, despite what men would like to believe (and what *I* would like them to believe), for the most part pussy is just pussy. Trust me, I've dealt with enough of it to know. At $300 to $350 an hour, most of my entertainers—who get two-thirds of that fee plus any tips they earn, and at this level, most guys tip—are going to feel well paid for their work, and most of my clients are going to feel like it was money well spent. But at $1,500 an hour, it's difficult for the client to be anything but disappointed, unless he's the kind of guy who can throw $1,500 around without flinching. And there just aren't enough of those guys around to really make a business.

Getting caught is always a concern in my line of work, but the business is not as risky as some people might think, as long as you're smart about it. In order for me to get caught, someone who has witnessed illegal activity, usually a client or a girl, has to turn me in. Since I'm never there when the illegal activity takes place, finding a witness can be very difficult. And since both the clients and the girls have participated in some illegal doings themselves, they aren't, generally speaking, so anxious to talk to the authorities. On top of that, I'm extremely careful about who I do business with on both sides of the transaction.

Usually, if a girl has worked before, if she has already established a reputation in the business —and these days every girl who has been around the block has her "reputation" posted on special peer review sites on the World Wide Web—you know it's safe to hire her. After all, no undercover cop would actually do the deed just to bust someone.

Besides, let's face it, the cops know we're out there. Everyone knows were out there. Prostitution is the oldest business in the world, and it's no secret that it exists all around us—in every state, in every city, in every country around the globe. When the cops arrest a girl for working, they usually just fill out a report, hold her for a bit, and then let her go. They have better things to do with their time than worry about who is screwing who.

Generally, as long as business stays low-key—and I've mastered the art of low-key business—people leave us alone, unless the cops are motivated to make a point. It happens every once in a while . . . they decide to make a show of how tough they are on crime, how they're working to clean up the streets and protect the children and all that. It happened to me several times in New York, where I used to run a brothel, and that's why I got out of the city. Giuliani had just become mayor, and he had promised during his campaign to clean up New York. Curbing all the conspicuous prostitution going on all over town became a top priority for the police department when he took office.

Of course, in the long run the effect was mostly cosmetic. The cops would make regular sweeps of businesses like my brothel, which was out in the open and easy to find, forcing them to shut down. Business calmed down for a while, but then it came back as strong as ever, just in a different way—on the Internet instead of the street corner. Giuliani only succeeded in driving it underground so that the taxpayers could pretend it wasn't happening all around them. (I heard he did the same thing with the homeless.)

I don't do business like that anymore. I don't have a physical location that cops can bust whenever they feel like it. I'm mobile, which makes me harder to find, and much more careful and discreet. Having to go underground was actually better for me and for a lot of people in this business. It forced us to become smarter. Now I'm making more money *and* I feel safer.

Still, I know that I'm never entirely safe. When that cop answered Zoe's phone, I didn't know how much danger I was in, but I knew I couldn't take the risk. I shut down my business. I took down my Web site and Internet ads, which is something I would do only in extreme situations, because it means my clients don't know how to find me. I thought the police might be able to trace me through the SIMM card in my cell phone, so I threw it out, which meant I lost all of my phone numbers. Thank god I have a good memory, especially when it comes to client info. Then I put what was left of my things in storage so I could travel light and so I wouldn't have anything on me to be used as evidence if it came to that.

Without two very important things—my cell, which was now in storage, and my computer, which I could only assume was in police custody—I can't work. My business is built around the idea that my identity must be protected at all times, so almost nothing is done in person. My clients, most of my girls even, know me only as a voice on the phone or a message in their in-boxes. I use a pseudonym and I try never to show my face. When something does need to be done in person, like exchanging money, I have assistants who act as go-betweens, which is another reason why it would be hard for the cops to pin something on me.

If I couldn't work, then there would be no cash coming in. I didn't want to go to my safety deposit box, because I was afraid someone could be waiting there for me. Call me paranoid, but you just never know. So I had to live off what I had on me. I found a quiet hotel room back in New Jersey and stayed put, just me and my dog, Max. I didn't go out or talk to a soul.

It's times like these when I usually decide to pick up and start my life over. Drop me down in the middle of any large to midsize city, and within days, I will be self-supporting. Within weeks, I will be on my way to setting up a profitable business.

But this time, even though I was risking getting caught, I didn't leave town. I don't know why I decided to do things differently. It went against everything I had ever learned about this business. For better or worse, I found a place to hide and waited to see what would happen.

CHAPTER 2

What $100,000 Can Buy You

It's no accident that I'm so good at picking up and starting over. I've had lots of practice at it, starting when I was very young, before I had any choice in the matter.

My earliest memory is from Korea, where I was born in the mid-1970s. My grandmother was beating me with a baseball bat. At least I think she was my grandmother. I was so young when I saw her last I don't really know for sure who she was.

My grandmother, my big sister—or at least someone I called "*Uhn-nee,*" which means "big sister" in Korean—and I all lived together in the back of a restaurant that sold hot dogs. We had only one room for the three of us to share, so we must have been poor. Grandmother was senile, so she couldn't really care for me. In fact, the only time I remember her paying attention to me at all was when she was beating me or telling me what to do. Big Sister was the one who looked after me, when she had the time. She was usually very busy cleaning, working in the restaurant, and taking care of Grandmother. I remember sometimes leaving the restaurant out of boredom and wandering the streets by myself for who knows how long.

Other memories from that time are still vivid in my mind. I remember eating one bowl of soup a day and cleaning, always cleaning. I'm a clean freak to this day, and I think that must be why. I especially remember one of my recurring childhood nightmares because I still have it sometimes: A normal-looking man is talking to me when, suddenly, he does a kind of somersault and turns into a vicious vampire wolf. Whenever I dream this, I wake up screaming, covered in sweat, and shaking with fear.

Eventually I ended up in an orphanage. I don't know if someone took me away because Grandmother was too sick or too old, or if she put me up for adoption herself, or if she sold me. It was the people at the orphanage who explained what had happened to my real parents. My mother, they said, had died in childbirth, and my father was in the military, always traveling, so I couldn't live with him. That was what they told me, but they offered no proof. Many years later, as an adult, I sat next to a Korean woman on a train and we started talking. It turned out that she had worked in an orphanage in Korea, so she knew how these things typically were handled. Back then there was no formal adoption process in the country, so everything was done on the black market. It wasn't considered normal for Korean people to give up their children, so stories were often made up to explain away the situation. You can't blame a mother for dying and leaving her child behind, so that was a popular excuse. Of course, some mothers do actually die in childbirth, so I've never really known whether to believe the story I was told or not.

I also remember being on an airplane with one or two other Korean kids. They must have been orphans too. We were on our way to America, although at the time I had no idea what was happening to me. I don't remember feeling scared exactly, just confused and out of place. When we landed, my new family was waiting for me at the airport gate—Mom, Dad, and my new big sister, Michelle, my new parents' natural daughter. That's when I got Teddy, my very first teddy bear, who meant so much to me that I've kept him to this day. I couldn't remember having ever been given anything before, so I was very excited by the concept of toys.

I was six years old, and my new home was in a very upscale town in suburban Connecticut. We lived in a huge house next to a large apple orchard near a pond. There was a guesthouse on our property, where a sweet couple lived with their baby. The husband was our groundskeeper, and he maintained all the land, which included a well-kept front yard, a huge backyard with trees, a swing set, and a sandbox, and, behind the guesthouse, the main stretch of orchards, which just went on and on. It was about as picturesque as you can get.

I don't remember arriving at my new home, but I do remember a dinner party we had a few days later in celebration of my arrival. Everyone was so big and so white. While sitting in the dining room, I wondered if there was going to be enough food for all of us or if we were going to have to eat our dog, Figi, who looked like a big hairy hot dog with little legs. It's funny what stays with you. People kept coming over to me and hugging and kissing me. I think they were family members; some may have been neighbors. Our neighborhood was a very friendly place.

Across the street from us lived the Addamses. I liked them so much I named the father in my new dollhouse after Mr. Addams. They had a pool in their backyard and threw great pool parties. Since I'd never really had friends before, I spent a lot of time at their house playing with their two kids, who were about my age. That is, until one day when we were playing doctor and one of them cut my nipple with a plastic knife while trying to perform "surgery" on me. That's the last time I remember being at their house, although the scar from where the real doctor stitched me up still reminds me of them.

I used to hear my mother gossiping about the Addams family. Mr. Addams, she said, was having an affair with his secretary. Later he divorced his wife and moved to some state that didn't enforce child support, or at least that's what the neighbors were saying.

A little farther down the road were the Millers. The husband

13

sold fancy cars all over the East Coast. I remember their house being creepy, but I think that's because it was the first place I ever babysat and someone had told me that story about the babysitter who gets spooked by a crank caller and when the police trace the call, they tell her, "It's coming from inside the house!" That story still sends chills down my spine.

Down near the pond, where we would go ice skating in the winter, was a newer development with just three houses. The one at the end of the road was a huge, modern house where the Yis lived. They were a Korean family, the only one around.

Mrs. Yi helped my mother a lot when I first arrived, since I spoke only Korean and my new family didn't have any other way to communicate with me. I continued to have nightmares, which caused me to cry and yell in my sleep. My mother grew so concerned that they began tape-recording me at night. Mrs. Yi would listen to the tapes and translate. Each night it was the same thing. I would scream about the monster, the vampire wolf. Years later I heard the tapes again, and they still frightened me.

Just like your typical American family, my parents divorced several years after my adoption. I was about nine then. I think my adoption had been a misguided attempt by my parents to save their marriage. Of course, it didn't work, and pretty soon Dad was on his third marriage (before my mom there had been the Brazilian wife), to a woman fifteen years younger than him.

My parents sold the house and the orchard and moved to separate parts of town at first, then to separate countries (Dad eventually settled in Europe with his new family). Michelle, who I was never very close to, chose to live with our dad. I ended up with Mom. And just like that, our not-so-happy family split down the middle; we all had to start over.

A few years later, when I was visiting my dad—who by that time had managed to create a perfect little life for himself with his perfect, young wife and their perfect new daughter—he told me what a disappointment I had been to all of them. When they had decided to adopt a child from Korea, they had been promised a baby. Then I showed up, already walking and talking and crying in my sleep. I caused them even more trouble after he and Mom split. By the time he told me this, I had run away a few times and Mom was having problems coping with me, all of which was getting expensive for him, since he still supported us. "I already paid $100,000 for you and I'm still paying," he told me.

It wasn't until later that I learned exactly what he meant. It had cost him $100,000 to adopt me and have me brought here from Korea. He had been skeptical about the whole idea from the beginning, but my mom's heart had been set on it. I have a feeling that he thought there were better things he could have done with his money, like taking a long vacation to Africa, which is what he and wife number three did with my college fund after it became obvious that I wasn't going to college.

I didn't talk to my father much after that. He isn't the type of person I would have chosen for a father anyway, if only a person could choose such things. He's rich, but not like the rich people I've met since leaving home. He has money because he comes from a rich family, not because he's earned it. He has never really worked, despite the fact that he went to an Ivy League school and had every advantage. Instead, he lives off the yearly allowance he gets from his own parents. How can you respect someone like that, someone who has never done anything for himself? I just knew I never wanted to be like him.

He used to keep an office in our house, which became the source of many jokes when I realized what an office was really supposed to be for. For him it wasn't a place where he did actual business, just somewhere he would disappear to, to read the paper, play the stock market, or simply hide out from his family whenever he felt like it. No one was allowed to bother him when he was in his office, and if we did, there was hell to pay.

Given that I never thought much of my father, I can't say I miss him. It wasn't my fault he decided to pay all that money for me and then got scammed. If someone steals your money, it's your own fault for not protecting yourself. That's what I've come to learn. His regrets are his own. When he told me that story of my adoption, all I could think was, At least I didn't come cheap. In fact, I wish they'd made him pay a whole lot more for me.

CHAPTER 3

Runaway

The first time I ran away from home, I was thirteen years old. Mom and I had been on our own for a while then. Not long after the divorce, she came into my room one morning and said, "It's time for a fresh start!" Soon after, we left Connecticut and moved into a sweet little house beside a river in a small town in Maine near the coast. The house wasn't as grand as our place in Connecticut, but we still had a nice piece of property and plenty of wealthy neighbors, so there is no reason to feel bad for us.

Connecticut had been bad enough, but in Maine, I was the only Asian kid in school. There was one black kid too, a boy who was a couple of years older than me, but that was it. Everyone else was white as far as the eye could see. When I first got to my new school, a bunch of kids made fun of me for looking different. It quickly became clear to me that the black kid and I were either going to be the most popular or the most unpopular kids around. There was no way to blend in, so we had to be one or the other.

Fortunately, I was able to make some friends and I got good grades. In sixth grade, my two best girlfriends and I all had a crush on the same boy, John, who was the school hunk. That year he asked me out at the school dance, and I gained instant popularity. Of course, once I got the popularity I wanted, I didn't need him anymore. (John was actually kind of boring, so I dumped him a month later.) I think I was born with the fear-of-boredom gene. I knew instinctively that small-town life wasn't for me. I was drawn to adventure at a very young age. One of my early heroes was Al Capone.

Mom had a hard time adjusting to life on her own almost from the start. I could tell that she didn't like being alone, and I know I was a handful. She had always been a bit New Agey, but she started to really get into things like psychic healing and channeling one's inner child. She tried to get me into these things too. She wanted me to talk about my memories of Korea and my dreams. At one point she even tried to help me track down my *"uhn-nee,"* my big sister who had taken care of me when I lived in Korea, but we never found her. The whole "making peace with your past" thing just wasn't for me anyway.

I think all that stuff was Mom's attempt to feel better about her life, but it didn't really work. She just got more and more depressed. One day she came to me and said she was checking herself into a private psychiatric hospital and I would be staying for a while with our neighbor, who was this woman I barely knew. It wasn't the neighbor's fault, and she probably meant well, but she and I didn't get along right from the start. I resented being stuck with her, and I acted out as often as I could. I started ditching school, just cutting a class or two at first, then whole days at a time. One day I wanted to go to a Def Leppard concert and the neighbor wouldn't let me go, but I just went anyway.

After the concert I returned to the neighbor's house. She was furious with me, but since she wasn't my mother, I didn't really care. I realized then that no one could stop me from doing what I wanted to do, at least not for long. Sometimes when I'd sneak out, someone would catch me, but other times, no one did. I learned that, if I just kept trying, eventually I'd get my way. One day I left the neighbor lady's house again without telling her and went to stay with a friend and her grandmother in Old Orchard Beach, which was a town on the coast, quite a ways from where we lived. That time I stayed away for a while.

Old Orchard Beach was a cheesy and slightly sleazy vacation town, not unlike Atlantic City only much smaller and sleepier. At one of the shops on the boardwalk, I met a boy from Argentina who was working there for the summer and fell for him on first sight. I wanted to spend all my time with him, so I ditched my friend and her grandmother to stay with him. When he told me he was leaving town soon, I asked him to take me with him, but he said no, probably because I insisted on staying a virgin. I was admittedly boy crazy back then, but my parents had instilled strong values in me (before the family fell apart, that is). I still considered myself a good girl, so I stuck to kissing and hand-holding. In my mind, running away didn't count as bad behavior because Mom had left me with someone who I couldn't stand and who couldn't stand me, so I didn't think I had a choice. After my crush left town, I didn't feel like going back to either my friend's or the neighbor lady's house. Stuck and with nowhere to go, I ended up sleeping on the beach with some other runaways.

I may have only been in junior high school (if I had been going to school, that is; eighth grade would end up being the highest grade I would complete), but I learned quickly that I could make it on my own. I found out that I could stay in abandoned houses or at the YWCA, where I met a bunch of kids who were following the Grateful Dead from town to town. The Dead was big back then, especially where I lived, and especially with the kinds of kids who ran away to go to concerts and stayed in YWCAs. I didn't really like the band's music, but I soon discovered that Deadheads always had acid. I also discovered that I could support myself by buying it in bulk from them and selling it to kids at the beach.

At first I would buy acid just for myself, one tab at a time when I wanted to get high and had the money, but then one of the Deadheads told me I could get a whole sheet of one hundred hits for just eighty dollars. That worked out to just eighty cents a hit, while the going rate for a single dose was five dollars. I suddenly thought, Holy shit, I can actually make money off of this! If I could just come up with enough cash to buy a whole sheet, then I would have enough to sell to my friends, pocket a little cash, and keep a tab for myself for free.

I think I was born with natural business instincts. I've learned a lot from various players, pimps, and dealers—the businessmen of my world—along the way, but I have been able to learn from them because I think I have a head for such things. (It's mostly been learning by watching, after all, since none of those guys were particularly good teachers.) I got it into my head that I had to come up with that eighty dollars one way or another, and then the idea just came to me: I'd sell fake stuff first to raise the cash. I got some blotter paper, borrowed a pizza cutter from a friend, and made what looked like a sheet of acid. Then I sold it to kids who were already fucked up on something so they wouldn't notice the difference. It worked like a charm.

I didn't make that much money selling acid, but in those days I didn't need much either. Just some food and play money. My time on my own in Old Orchard Beach was like one big, long party. It wasn't like running away to somewhere scary (like when I ended up in New York City a few years later). I could always find kids to hang out with—rock 'n' roll boys, other runaways. We'd find abandoned buildings to meet in or just gather on the beach. Of course, it couldn't last forever. It was a great place to be in the summertime, but as soon as it started to turn cold, the party ended.

When I finally tried to go back to the neighbor lady's place, she was pissed. She locked me out and told my mom that I couldn't stay with her anymore. My mom, who was still in the psychiatric hospital, had been freaking out. Since there was no one else to take care of me, and probably no one who could handle me, she arranged for me to stay at the hospital too; it had a youth program for troubled teenagers. The counselors there diagnosed me as having a substance abuse problem, and I was given a room that I shared with another problem kid.

Even though it was technically a mental hospital, the place was more like a country club or a spa. It was surrounded by this huge wooded park, and every room had gorgeous views of the trees and grass and hills. The food was phenomenal, and there were all sorts of things to do, like swimming, board games, or even just hanging out with the other kids. Except for the fact that it was a hospital, it was probably the most normal part of my entire childhood after my parents split up.

It cost something like $600 a day, however, and my dad was footing the entire bill, which, of course, doubled when I showed up. My room was nice, and most of the staff were cool, fun twentysomethings fresh out of college. They used to take us on trips to the beach or to the mountains. I was happy to be back with my mom, so even though I was in trouble, I was glad that things worked out that way. I loved it there and would have stayed forever or, at least, until my mom was ready to leave. If only they would have let me.

I got to see a psychiatrist while I was there, and I actually liked that too. His name was Stanley, and he used to pace back and forth while we talked. He had all sorts of nervous tics, like tugging at his long mustache. I liked that he wasn't perfect and that he didn't bother to try to hide his tics. Everything about Stanley was just obvious and out on the table, no pretense. I remember thinking he would make a good dad. There was another psychiatrist there too, a woman who dressed like a schoolteacher from *Little House on the Prairie*. Everyone could tell that Stanley had a crush on her. The other kids and I would tease him about it and he would turn bright red.

My mom and the people at the hospital may not remember it this way, but I tried my best to be good while I was there because I really wanted to stay. Stanley was a good listener, and I had fun with the other kids. I got to see my mom regularly. But somehow, even with my best intentions, things started to go wrong. One day my mom found a pack of cigarettes in my room. I was still only fourteen, so smoking was a big deal to her.

"It's not mine, Mom. It belongs to my girlfriend," I told her, which was the truth, but she didn't believe me. She made me smoke the entire pack right there in front of her. That was the first time I ever smoked, a habit I still have to this day. I can't really blame my mom for most of how my life has turned out, but I definitely put smoking on her.

That was strike one. Strike two was when I took a beer up to my room. That time it was mine, but I never intended to drink it, or not all of it anyway. I just wanted to wash my hair with it. I read in a magazine that it was good to wash your hair in beer once a month. My girlfriend and I had a few sips each and then tried it out on our hair. It seemed to work; our hair was totally clean. Afterward, I threw the empty can under my bed, where my mom later found it and confronted me. Again, I told her the truth about what happened. I may have done some bad things, but I was actually a pretty honest kid. I just wasn't the kind of kid people readily believed. I had only been at the hospital for a couple of months, and Mom already saw me as both a smoker and a drinker. Things were not looking good for me.

I probably could have gotten away with both offenses—after all, a lot of kids try cigarettes and a few sips of beer—but the last straw was really when one of the young guys on staff decided he liked me. He was one of the group who'd take us on trips, and he used to hold my hand when we went places even though I was a teenager and obviously didn't need any help crossing the street. He'd also come into my room at bedtime to kiss me good night. I kind of liked the attention and didn't really think that what we were doing was all that wrong, but when my mom and the rest of the staff found out what was happening, that was my strike three.

I was out: dismissed for having "sexual relations," if you could even call it that. My mom didn't stick up for me at all. She just agreed that it would be best if I left, quickly and quietly.

I wasn't the only one who had to leave. The counselor who liked to hold my hand was fired and told he could never work in the mental health care field again. I can definitely say that it wasn't worth it for me, but I honestly hadn't known things would turn out like that. It probably wasn't worth it for him either (all I let him do was hold my hand and tuck me in at night), but he must have known how much trouble he could get into. I still wonder why he would risk so much to get so little in return. I'll never understand why men are willing to risk so much just for a little affection.

I didn't realize it at the time, but I wouldn't see much more of my mom after that and I'd never live with her again. She stayed at the hospital receiving treatment for depression for quite some time after I left. Once in a while she'd come visit me wherever I happened to be at the time, but we never really connected. I used to call her the "robot mom" because she was always so intent on "following the rules." Whose rules, I don't know exactly—society's, I guess—but I obviously didn't live up to her standards for good behavior.

After the hospital I ended up in a group home way up in northern Maine, which was practically the wilderness. It wasn't nearly as nice as the hospital, but there was a boy there I liked named Dominik. Practically my first day there, he became my boyfriend, even though we didn't really know each other that well. He was fun, everyone liked him, and he was easy to talk to, all of which made life at the group home bearable for a while. That is until he ran away with a big guy named Don. The news that Dom and Don had split traveled fast around the home. It traveled even faster when the police finally caught up to them. Word came back that Dominik had died after he fell off a construction site during their run.

After Dominik was gone, I couldn't take it anymore. I was sad to lose him, but what was even worse was that everyone in the whole place was so upset about it all the time. It was way too depressing to stay there. I decided that if Dominik could do it, I could too, so I ran away. But my freedom didn't last long. I got arrested for stealing cigarettes and ended up in another youth center, and this one was run by the state. It was the worst place I'd been so far, but I remember it fondly because it was there that I became best friends with Natasha, who would come to shape the rest of my short-lived childhood.

I still remember the first time I saw Natasha. It was actually at the group home where Dominik and I were living. Her younger brother lived there, and one afternoon she came to visit him. As soon as she walked in the room, all the boys stopped what they were doing and just stared at her. All the girls did too. She was just so gorgeous, it was impossible to ignore her. She had this long blond hair and a curvy body like a Barbie doll's. She looked older than the rest of us, even though she was just a year older than me. She could knock people off their feet with just one piercing look, and she knew it too. She was powerful and charming. She flashed me a big smile when she caught me looking at her, and I couldn't help but like her.

I didn't talk to her that day, but not long afterward I got my chance. When I arrived at the state youth center, she was already living there. Maine may be a big state, but there are so few people that, whether I was on the streets or in one of the state-run centers, there were familiar faces everywhere I went. There just weren't that many "problem kids" in Maine, and as a result, there were only so many places we could end up. In that way we made up our own kind of extended dysfunctional family.

"You must know my brother!" Natasha said to me when she realized where I'd come from. She made me feel immediately comfortable, and I latched on to her after that. She didn't seem to mind. I think she liked me right away too, probably because I bothered her less than the other kids did. Besides being beautiful, she was much wiser and more worldly than the rest of us, so kids were always asking her advice about this, what she thought about that, if she liked such-and-such person/band/outfit. And her opinion reigned—whatever she thought was considered cool. She always knew what to say to people and was too sweet to tell anyone to leave her alone. Everyone looked up to her, including me, but I was best at playing it cool.

All the kids at the youth center had to have jobs, so Natasha and I got jobs working together in the kitchen. It was our responsibility to clean up after dinner. The whole place looked like a summer camp. Kids lived in seven or eight cottages grouped together—boys on one side, girls on the other—in a clearing surrounded by woods. Each evening we would carry a big plastic bucket from cottage to cottage collecting leftover food to be brought back to the kitchen and thrown away. There were so many rules at that place and so little to do that this was one of the highlights of our very dull days.

One day, while we were making our rounds of the cottages, Natasha looked at me and, for no apparent reason, said, "Let's see if we can make it to the woods!"

I paused for a moment and then smiled in agreement. We were bored and it was something to do. We dropped our buckets and made a break for it, running as fast as we could toward the tree line before someone could catch us.

I didn't really think we would make it very far, but to my surprise, we did. Once we made it into the woods, we didn't stop. We just kept on running and running until we were out of breath. We stopped to rest in an area near a few houses. By that time, we were already pretty far away from the center.

Once we finally stopped running, neither of us really knew what to do next. We knew that the center would send the police after us as soon as they noticed we were gone, so we were afraid to venture out of the woods. The police would likely be checking the roads, so we didn't want to go near them. We also didn't want to walk by the houses, which was the direction we needed to go if we wanted to get farther away from the center, because someone might see us. "Let's just stay here for a while," Natasha finally decided. "When it gets dark enough that no one can see us, then we can leave."

As it grew darker and darker, I began to get nervous. Suddenly our game didn't seem like so much fun anymore. I think Natasha must have been nervous too, but she didn't let on. Instead, to pass the time, we quietly sang our favorite songs from the radio to each other—songs by Melissa Etheridge, Whitney Houston, George Michael. We sang songs about relationships and betrayal, desire and passion, all things that we were too young to really understand. Our absolute favorite was "Against All Odds" by Phil Collins. It became like a theme song after that because we felt like practically everything that was good in our lives happened "against all odds." We sang it to each other that night, I think, as a way of saying we'd stay friends forever, no matter what, even if we got caught or separated, both of which were pretty likely. Kids in state facilities were always getting transferred or released or moved to a different kind of program, so even though I recognized kids everywhere I went, it was hard to keep any really strong ties to anyone. Natasha and I didn't want that to happen to us. That song meant so much to us that I still remember most of the lyrics: "We've shared the laughter and the pain, and even shared the tears / You're the only one who really knew me at all . . . Oh take a look at me now, well there's just an empty space / And you coming back to me is against all odds and that's what I've got to face."

We must have stayed in the woods for hours. Finally, when it was dark, Natasha whispered to me, "Let's get out of here."

We crept quietly past the houses and down to the nearest road. Our plan was to walk, or hitch a ride if we could, toward Natasha's hometown, which was not far away, and meet up with some of her childhood friends. So that's what we did.

The first thing we did when we hooked up with Natasha's

friends was get our hands on some good clothes and makeup. We knew that we should leave Maine as soon as possible, since there would be people out looking for us by then, and the farther away we got, the safer we'd be. But we never got to have much fun at the youth center, so all we wanted to do that night was party to celebrate our newfound freedom. Natasha's friends were having a bonfire on the beach, and we couldn't turn that down. When I look back now, I realize they were mostly a group of high school deadbeats, but at the time, they seemed like the coolest people I'd ever met.

When we woke up the next morning, I don't think Natasha, who was really our leader and made all the big decisions for both of us, really knew what to do next. "We've got to keep moving farther away from the center" was all she said, so we started hitchhiking. Through a combination of rides and walking, we made it to Massachusetts by nighttime. We were near Boston when a man stopped to pick us up. "If you want to come back to my place with me tonight, we can have something to eat and then get a good night's sleep," he said. "I'm heading out early tomorrow morning, so I'll take you where you want to go then."

Since we hadn't eaten all day, we happily agreed. The man drove us to his house, where he made us dinner, which we ate ravenously, and then Natasha and I fell asleep together in his bed.

It was the middle of the night when I woke up, not sure where I was or what was going on. As the haze of sleep lifted, I realized that the bed was shaking and that must have been what had startled me out of my sleep. When I opened my eyes, I saw that the man was right next to me, lying on top of Natasha. She wasn't looking at me, but I could still see by the faint light coming in through a nearby window that her eyes were filled with tears. I knew something very bad was happening, but I was so scared that I just closed my eyes and pretended to be asleep. I could hear the man grunting but not a sound from Natasha. She was dead silent the whole time.

As I was lying there wishing the man would leave us alone, I felt a hand drift over to my leg. I was still pretending to be asleep as he began to run his big, clumsy hand up and down my thigh. I had no idea what to do, so I just froze. Suddenly, I felt Natasha knock his hand away and hiss at him in a harsh tone that meant business: "No! Not her!"

The man stopped touching me after that, and I cracked open one eye to see if he was mad at Natasha. But he didn't seem to be angry at all. He was actually grinning as he grabbed Natasha's T-shirt, which she still had on, and yanked it up to reveal her breasts. He squeezed them roughly, and I could tell that it hurt her. He pinched her nipples and continued grunting until he seemed to run out of breath. Moments later, he fell fast asleep alongside Natasha, who was crying softly. Not sure what else to do, I reached over and grabbed her hand. She didn't look at me, but she did tenderly touch my arm and whispered to me: "Everything's okay. Just get some sleep."

I wanted to trust Natasha, but I couldn't sleep. I lay there quietly for a while, too scared to move, but the longer I did, the worse I felt. I was afraid the man might wake up, and I didn't think we wanted to be there when that happened. I looked over at Natasha and could tell that she wasn't asleep either, so I waved my hand at her to get her attention and then motioned toward the door. We got up quietly and tiptoed out of the room.

Before we left, we took a few things that we needed: a half-empty pack of cigarettes and about ten dollars that we found lying on the kitchen counter. That was a lot of money to us at the time, so we were pretty psyched about it. When we got outside, we took off running until we couldn't see the man's house anymore. We made it to a highway and decided to try hitchhiking again. This time we weren't going to let whoever picked us up take us just anywhere. We had decided on a destination, and it was there or nothing. We were heading for New York City.

CHAPTER 4

The Pimp and Ho Game

Despite our big-city plans, we made it only as far as Worcester, Massachusetts, that night. We were heading south, which was the right direction, but if you've ever been to Worcester, you know it's no substitute for New York City. It's a dull and ugly place filled with highways and low-income houses. There was a mall and a concert arena, but not much else of excitement for two teenage girls. The only reason we ended up staying there for several months is because we were able to make friends quickly and get jobs, two things we sorely needed.

For the first couple of weeks we were in Worcester, we stayed with a girl Natasha knew. The girl wasn't going to let us stay forever, however, so we had to make some new connections. In any town, kids who are bored and looking for trouble will eventually find one another, or at least that has been my experience. That's how Natasha and I became friends with members of the local Puerto Rican gang. When we were bored, we'd walk up and down Main Street looking for something to do. The street passed right by the projects where a lot of Puerto Rican kids lived, and they'd do the same thing. "Hey, *niñas*!" they'd yell at us, and if we had nothing better to do, we'd answer them.

The gang was all too happy to adopt us for a while. It never hurts to have two cute young girls following you around. Some of them had cars, and we didn't mind being their arm candy as long as they'd drive us places once in a while. One of them started seeing Natasha, and when we had to leave her friend's place, he let us move in with him. We needed some money, so one of the guys took us to a local strip club, where he said we could make some easy cash. He introduced us to the owner, and pretty soon we had jobs. We danced for a flat fee of $150 a day. The owner would take all our tips, but I never questioned this practice because I understood instinctively how things like that worked. It was his place and he was entitled to make the rules since he was taking all the risk, especially with girls as young as us working there. I was fifteen at the time, and he must have known that Natasha and I were underage, he just didn't care. That guy was my first real boss. I knew even then that someday I wanted to be the one who was in the position to make all the rules.

After about a month, Natasha and I were getting used to life on our own. None of this had been our plan—we never really had a plan in the first place—but the longer we were out in the world, the more sure we were that we never wanted to go back to any state facility. We had both hated the center, and life now was pretty entertaining by comparison. Everything was an adventure, and we did it all together. We always worked the same shifts at the strip club so we could keep an eye on each other. When we had nothing better to do, we'd go to the park and find a baseball game to watch. We'd sit in the stands, pick a side to root for, and make friends with whoever was there just for fun. Even if we sometimes didn't know where we were going to live or how we'd be able to eat, we weren't all that scared to be on our own. It never really occurred to us how vulnerable we were out in the world at our age with no one to look out for us but each other.

When we were together, Natasha and I made a big impression. She was pale and curvy with that thick blond hair that hung all the way to her waist, and I was dark and waifish—thin as a rail, really—with hair just as long only jet black and silky. When we couldn't get one of the guys to drive us, we had to walk wherever we wanted to go. But as long as the weather was good, we didn't mind. We had fun counting the honks and whistles we got along the way.

One day, we'd set out on one of our long walks to the mall when we came across a trio of people—a man and two girls, one black and one white, who both looked about eighteen. Natasha stopped when she saw them and whispered to me with a giggle, "See that guy over there? That guy's a pimp!"

"Nuh-uh," I replied. "That's no pimp."

I'd seen a pimp before, in Old Orchard Beach, the first time I'd run away. He drove a beat-up old Toyota and hustled along a short stretch of the boardwalk with one or two tired-looking girls always in tow. The guy standing a few yards away from us looked nothing like that. He was slick and put together, like he had cash, and he wore a Fendi suit. I could tell it was Fendi because both his pants and jacket were completely covered in the brand's trademark repeating F pattern, which, before that moment, I had seen only on women's handbags. He also sported more gold than Flavor Flav—it was all over his wrists, his fingers, and there was a big pile of it around his neck. The car parked nearby, which had to be his because he kept moving back and forth between it and the two girls, was a beige Mercedes.

Natasha just laughed at how naïve I was. I don't know how she knew what they were, but there was no doubt in her mind that this guy was a pimp and those were his hos, even though I didn't believe her. She could hardly take her eyes off the three of them. She just watched, fixated, as I tried to sort out what they were doing there.

"Well, if you're so interested, I'll go find out," I finally said, marching past her before she could say anything.

The Fendi guy's back was toward me as I approached. I ignored the two girls and walked straight up to him. "Are you a pimp?" I demanded in my most authoritative voice.

"Who wants to know?" he responded, whirling around to look at me. I had snuck up on him, and I could tell by his face that he was a little taken aback by the question. But as soon as he got a good look at me, his expression relaxed. He probably weighed twice what I did, and he was at least half a foot taller than me, so I clearly wasn't a threat to him. And it was obvious that I wasn't a cop or even a concerned citizen trying to give him a hard time. I was just some young girl who didn't know any better than to talk to a guy like him on the street.

He grinned and immediately started chatting me up. "You're a pretty one, aren't you? What's a lovely girl like you doing out here on a day like this? Shouldn't you be relaxing somewhere nice with somebody pampering and taking care of you?" Then he noticed Natasha coming toward us.

"Is that your friend?" he asked, raising his eyebrows just slightly as he looked past me at her.

"Yes," I replied.

He paused for a moment to take us both in and then said in a voice soaked with charm, "If you girls are looking for something to do, why don't you hang out with me? I bet we could have some fun."

"We don't want to hang out here. It's boring here." I was still doing all the talking, even though Natasha had joined us by then.

"We could go somewhere," he suggested. "I've got some wheels."

"Where are we going?" Natasha finally spoke up.

"Where do you want to go?"

"How about New York?" she asked.

"I could take you to New York."

"We've wanted to go to New York forever, but we haven't been able to find a ride."

"Well then, I guess we've got to go," Fendi guy said with a big smile spreading across his face.

The guy's name, we soon learned, was Julio. He wanted to pick up a friend on the way, and he said we had to leave right away, probably before we wised up and changed our minds about going anywhere with him. We were game for anything, as long as we ended up in New York, so we hopped in his car and turned on the radio. We were finally on our way to the one place we had really wanted to go.

Julio's friend was named Paolo Dante, but everyone just called him Dante. I liked him as soon as I met him. He was hot and he drove a little black Mercedes, which we thought was way cooler than Julio's ride. He didn't seem as excited about our trip as Julio was, but he agreed to come along, and, after we begged, he let us ride in his car. We set off in a two-car caravan: Natasha and I rode along with Dante and his girlfriend in the black Mercedes, and Julio and one of his girls were in the beige one. Natasha and I didn't really care if Dante was happy about the whole thing or not. We just thought we were finally riding in style.

After we'd been driving for a while, both cars turned off the highway. We were going to make a stopover on our way to New York, we were told, which was Julio's attempt to turn Natasha and me out. Not that we understood it at the time, but Julio knew what he was doing. He knew that New York was too big and too hard a place to teach us the ropes with all the action that was always going on, so he thought he'd ease us into things while also making some quick cash in the process.

When we got to some town in Connecticut that Julio seemed to know, we all pulled over by the side of the road. Dante didn't want any part of Julio's plan, so he took off, leaving us with Julio. While we sat in his car, Julio schooled us on what to do. The first thing he told us was that, if any cops came around, we should never tell them our real names. My name for the evening was to be China White. I was twenty-three years old and spoke almost no English. He gave me some bogus address, like 123 Main Street or something, which was where I was supposed to tell them I lived if the cops arrested me and wrote up a report. He quizzed us both on the info until we knew it cold and then put Natasha and me in some little dresses and threw us out on a dark street corner by ourselves.

I was scared and held Natasha's hand. We just stood there, unsure of what to do next, until Julio's girl stuck her head out the car window and yelled at us. "Run!" she screamed. So we did, hiding behind a building until two cars came racing up. I don't know if it was the noise Julio's girl was making that drew them or if this was just a neighborhood that they patrolled regularly, but the two cars turned out to be unmarked cop cars. It was a tough break for Julio, because he was still nearby. We all got arrested, and we had only been there for about half an hour.

That was my very first time in jail. We had to stay there until morning, when someone came to let us out. I don't know why we got to leave. Maybe someone bailed us out, or maybe they didn't have anything to charge us with. Either way, I didn't ask questions. I just signed the papers the cops put in front of me—China White, just like I'd been told—and then left with Natasha and Julio.

We drove to a nearby motel, where we got a room. Things started looking up when Natasha and I realized that Dante was already there, in the room next door. He and his girlfriend had had a nice quiet night together and were ordering breakfast when we showed up. He laughed his ass off when he saw us. It was like he was telling Julio, "I told you so, I told you not to mess with these girls."

Still, Julio wasn't giving up. He told me to clean myself up and then sent me to a room down the hall where some guy was waiting. I don't know how or when Julio made arrangements with him, but I think it was the manager of the motel. He was a sweaty, middle-aged Indian man who smelled like stale spices. As soon as I walked in the door, he started touching me without saying a word. I was still a virgin, so the whole thing grossed me out. The instant he pulled down his pants and I caught a glimpse of his dick, I threw up all over him.

I ran straight back to Dante's room, and when he heard what happened, he just couldn't stop laughing. Unfortunately, he was the only one who reacted that way. The guy I threw up on was pissed. Julio was pissed too, but he sent one of his other girls to make it up to the guy so I was off the hook. I don't think Natasha was as lucky as I was. She and Julio came into Dante's room, and I realized right away that they must have been alone together.

Natasha never said anything to me about what she and Julio had been doing, just like we never talked about what the guy who picked us up outside of Boston had done to her. I knew better than to press her for details. The kids I met in group homes or state facilities just didn't ask each other questions like that. We all knew from experience that the answers were never good, so it was like an unwritten rule among runaways and rejects not to talk about how you got there.

Natasha was no exception. She talked very little about her past. The only thing she would talk about was her little brother, and I gathered from what she said that she had taken care of him and defended him when they lived at home together. Defended him from what, I'm not sure, but I imagine her parents were not nice people. She treated me the same way she'd treated him, like someone she needed to look out for and shelter from an ugly world. No matter what was happening to us, she'd always say to me, "Don't worry, it's going to be okay." But I understood more than she thought. When you spend every hour of the day with one person for months and months at a time, you get pretty good at reading her. After Julio and Natasha came into the room that day, Natasha was distant and wouldn't look me in the eye. I knew that meant something bad had happened between them, and I could guess what it was.

Later that day we all packed into the cars again and headed

south. When we finally made it to New York City, I could hardly believe it. It was nighttime as we drove across the bridge into Manhattan, and the skyline was all lit up. I thought it was the most beautiful place I'd ever seen in my life. We drove through Times Square, with its flashing marquees, big bright billboards, and crowds of people everywhere. We drove past cross-dressers and trannies walking the streets as if they owned them. At a stoplight, I looked out the window and saw a black guy in a T-shirt that read "I ♥ NEW YORK." Below the T-shirt he wore a pair of sneakers and nothing else. His dick was just hanging out there for all to see. I laughed and elbowed Natasha to make sure she saw it too. I knew then and there that this was a place without any rules, where you could do whatever you wanted to do, be whoever you wanted to be. I fell in love with the city that night.

Even though it was late and we had just gotten to town, Julio had the idea that he should put Natasha and me to work right away. Typical pimp, all he could think about was the cash he was going to make off of us.

He drove us straight to the West Forties, which was one of the hottest centers of the city's thriving sex trade back then. This was the late eighties, before Times Square got its tourist-friendly makeover, when the pimps and the hos owned the streets. Everywhere you looked there were girls (or guys dressed as girls) walking the streets in their best getups—boas and big hair, stockings and lingerie, superhigh heels with attitudes to match. The pimps all had amazing rides: Rolls-Royces, Bentleys, or Jags. They wore colorful suits and crazy hats and would hang out on the corners or drive around in their cars to check on their "wares," while the girls sauntered from one end of the block to the other. Both the girls and their pimps were draped in gold and diamonds and seemed to pride themselves on their outfits—the wilder the better. It was as if they were peacocks engaged in some sort of strange mating ritual. I think the pimps and hos dressed up for one another more than for the tricks. No one had anywhere better to be, anything better to do, and no one was hiding. If you were a guy in from out of town looking for some company, all you had to do was drive west through Times Square and there you'd find a great show, as well as an all-you-can-eat buffet of company just waiting for you to choose from.

Julio was driving, and he was clearly familiar with this neighborhood. He pulled over right in the thick of things and, without ceremony, told us to take off our shorts so that all we had on were our T-shirts and G-strings.

"I don't want you running away from me," he said as he waited for us to strip down. "You don't want to be running around town in your underwear, so best to stay close to the car."

He gave us some stockings to put on and then shooed us out onto the street. We didn't even get close to attracting any customers, because as soon as we stepped outside, the other pimps in the neighborhood spotted us. It was their territory, and we were fresh meat that they were ready to claim for themselves. Several of them started walking toward us. It looked like it was going to be a battle to see who could devour us first.

What followed was a chase scene that I can hardly believe actually happened. It was like something from a bad slapstick comedy. It was warm enough outside that Natasha and I didn't mind being in our underwear too much. Natasha, who was always more aware of what was going on than I was, grabbed my hand as soon as she saw the men coming toward us. Despite Julio's efforts to make us flight proof, we took off running down the block. Julio took off after us, causing a couple of other pimps to take up the chase as well. We darted in between people and parked cars, ducked into the driver's side of one car that was unlocked, then jumped out the passenger side as soon as one of the pimps reached the door. I was so skinny then that the stockings Julio gave me kept falling down as I ran, and I almost ended up face-first on the pavement. Natasha and I were laughing the whole time. It seemed like a great game to us, but who knows how it would have ended if Dante hadn't driven up. It probably wouldn't have been pretty.

Dante is the only pimp I ever knew who had a conscience. He was disgusted by what Julio was trying to do to us, so as soon as Julio took off running, Dante jumped in the car to come get us. He slowed down just long enough for us to hop in the backseat and then drove away, leaving Julio and all the other pimps behind. He drove us straight out of town and didn't stop until we were back in Massachusetts. Our big trip to New York, and we didn't even get to spend the night.

I am not a pimp.

I mention this now because I don't want people thinking that these early experiences turned me into what I am today. I did learn from the pimps and hos I met along the way, but, mostly, I learned how *not* to be.

I have seen firsthand how pimps operate and why girls follow their lead. Why would any girl want to be some pimp's ho? Because she gets to live her life by a different set of rules, and a pimp knows how to make a girl feel special, when he wants to. A pimp will tell you you're gorgeous, you're sexy, you're like no one else in the world. Once he's got your attention, he'll say something like "Why wouldn't you want to use what you have to make some money? It's a gift, after all, and it's something people want. It's what makes you somebody." Then he'll take you to fancy places, dress you up in fancy clothes, introduce you to fancy people, and make you feel like you belong somewhere in this world. If you don't look too closely or for too long, the world that pimps offer their girls looks pretty glamorous. And what other choice do these girls really have? Young girls, poor girls, stupid girls, runaways like Natasha and me—there aren't many glamorous options for girls like that. There aren't a lot of not-so-glamorous options either.

There were some famous pimps around then that everyone in that world knew about. Like Diggy, a West Coast pimp who was always ten to twelve girls deep. He kept that many girls by making them believe it was a privilege to work for him. He made girls fill out an application to be with him, and if he accepted their company, they had to make appointments to see him once a month (guess what they did during those appointments). He also enforced a strict dress code and a diet-and-exercise regimen so that his girls would always look amazing, which they did. But they were locked down tight, with almost no leeway to do anything without his permission. And their quota was $1,000 a day.

There was also Candy Mac, an NYC pimp who was also always ten to twelve deep and who called his girls the "Mac Attitudes." He would marry his girls after ten years of commitment, and he actually *loved* them. Of course, he didn't divorce the old ones before he married a new one, so his "family" just kept getting bigger and bigger. And strangely, they did seem like one big, happy family. I think it helped that he chose girls who were bisexual so they were into each other as much as they were into him. And he did take care of them. His girls drove nice cars and wore nice clothes, furs, and jewelry. When they were working, he'd drive a big pimped-out van that had a place in the back where the girls could change, rest up, or chill out in between customers. He was a natural-born player, and I liked that about him.

There were all kinds of pimps around then, and different pimps played different games. Some would say sweet things to lure in girls; others were blatant dogs. Either way, most pimps were losers. The whole deal with pimps is that they really only protect you from other pimps. The work of finding customers and keeping safe during appointments is mostly done by the girls themselves, so if they were just smart about it, they didn't really need a pimp at all. That's why a pimp has to be smooth talker, to make a girl believe the lie that she can't live without him. That's what makes me hate pimps. They prey on the weak because their shit wouldn't work on anyone else. They're nothing without their girls, but they never let the girls know it. I mean, really, a pimp without hos is no pimp at all. A pimp will charm a girl just long enough to convince her that she belongs to him, then he convinces her that she's worthless without him. She's not much more than property after that. And the worst part is, I easily could have become one of those girls or maybe even like one of those pimps, which would have been even worse.

The title of "pimp" is a joke in my world. My friends tease me about it, and the boys who work for me laughingly call themselves my "pimp assistants." It's funny only because it's the opposite of what I am. A pimp takes all a girl's money. He thinks he owns her. The pimps I've met never take me seriously, even now—no matter how much more money I make than them—because they don't take any women seriously. I don't have time for such people, and back then I had time for them only because I didn't know any better and I needed them to survive.

Even the title of "madam" is tongue-in-cheek. The old definition of a madam was something like a girl's wrangler and den mother. She took care of her girls, kept them working and in line, often living with them in a house where they all did their business. But I think, if a girl needs to be taken care of like that, then she shouldn't be working at all and she definitely shouldn't be working for me.

I'm a businesswoman. An entrepreneur. I offer a service and give women an opportunity to profit from my name and reputation and from my clientele, who trust me. My job is to keep both the clients and the ladies safe, to manage the business so that it benefits everyone involved, and to market our services to the right people. Women choose for themselves if they want to work for me. *They* come to *me*.

When I'm trying to explain my work to people in the outside

world who have no context for understanding it, I tell them it's like being an agent. I know the ins and outs of this business. I know what girls need to do to make money. I know what the terms should be. I know good clients who want these services, and I do my best to connect the right girls with the right clients. The one big difference between me and most talent agents is that I never represent a girl exclusively, which means that a girl who works for me can also work for other services, or even for herself if she can pull it off. I don't own the rights to anyone, and why would I want to? I need to constantly bring in new blood in order to keep my clients happy, so I don't want to be responsible for any girl and her entire livelihood.

I never pick up anyone off the street and con her into working for me like Julio tried to do. I never sweet-talk anyone (and talk is one of the pimps' best weapons—they pride themselves on their verbal stylings, otherwise known as bullshit). And I *never* use underage girls. Dante was the same way. Underage girls were not his thing, but, like I said, Dante was not like other pimps.

After we left New York, Dante drove us straight back to Boston, where he lived. Natasha and I actually complained. We were so stupid back then. We had spent all that time trying to get to New York, and we couldn't believe he was taking us back to where we'd come from already. We had no idea how lucky we were.

Dante had a girl working for him named Kayla, and he took us to her house to stay. Kayla was probably no more than eighteen or nineteen years old, but she loved to mother us. She used to tell us when to brush our teeth and clean up after ourselves. She'd make us breakfast and find us outfits to wear. It was kind of like we were playing house.

Julio left us alone after that, even though it was no secret where we were. "He just doesn't want to look bad," Kayla explained. Julio knew that, if he came to get us, Dante would probably just steal us back. It was one thing to get stolen from in New York, where no one knew him, but a pimp never wants to get stolen from on his own turf and he definitely doesn't want to get stolen from twice. That would just make him appear weak, and for a pimp, it's all about reputation. Julio looked like a real loser already, having gone to New York with us in his possession and returned empty-handed.

If Kayla was like our mother, then Dante was definitely our daddy. I thought he was the coolest guy I'd ever met, and I developed a mad crush on him. He was way into music and got me into groups like 2 Live Crew, which were totally different from the Phil Collins songs Natasha and I used to listen to. I wrote him silly little love letters and even offered to work for him. I would have done anything to please him. Thank god he didn't take me up on any of my offers. He knew I was a virgin, and even though I'm sure he didn't have any illusions about how long my innocence was going to last given the company I kept, he just couldn't stomach being the one to corrupt me. In fact, I think he was a little bit afraid of me. Whenever I tried to flirt with him, he'd say something like, "If you keep talking to me like that, you're going to get me arrested," and then he'd walk away.

Natasha was a different story. She was older, only by a year, but to everyone around us it seemed like the age difference was much bigger. At five feet six, she was a few inches taller than me, and she had developed early; she had the body of a woman, while I looked more like a flat-chested little girl. Besides which, she was more experienced than me, and it showed. She was no virgin, and she made it clear that she really wanted to work. She told Dante, "I'm going to do it eventually no matter what you say, so why don't you just let me do it for you?" She just kept bugging him about it. Finally, he gave in. I guess he figured she'd be safer working for him than for anyone else.

Natasha was like that. She was fascinated by the lives of pimps and hos, and she was also very stubborn. Once she got an idea in her head, there was no one who could talk her out of it. And she took to the job like she had been doing it forever. You might even say she was a natural. At least that was the impression that Kayla, Dante, and Natasha gave me. It was about the time Natasha started working that they began to leave me out of things. I remember a lot of dinners in the apartment by myself, and since I couldn't cook, that meant eating lots and lots and lots of Ramen noodles.

Soon Dante was sending Natasha on appointments out of town. I remember feeling really left out when she and Kayla flew to California for a convention while I stayed home by myself. It was mostly boredom that I had been trying to escape when I ran away from the youth center, but there I was, stuck in a place with absolutely nothing to do once again. And even worse, now I had no one to talk to.

It was at that convention that they met Wesley, a computer nerd who had gone to MIT and made a fortune by the time he was thirty. When they met him, he was no longer a whiz kid, just a really smart, rich guy in his early thirties who was already bored with his life. Naturally, he fell in love with Natasha instantly.

I don't know what Wesley said to Natasha and Kayla exactly— probably something about what a great place he had and how much money he would throw around to entertain them—but when they got home, they couldn't wait to tell me the news.

"We're moving," Kayla said, as if that was clearly an exciting thing. I didn't know why we wanted or needed to go anywhere else, but Wesley had agreed to take all three of us in. I didn't ask how that negotiation took place. I assume that it was one of Natasha's conditions that we come along, and, from the beginning, Wesley let Natasha do whatever she wanted. The whole thing just seemed like a new adventure to me. Even Dante didn't question the arrangement. In fact, he seemed happy that we were going to be someone else's responsibility from now on.

Wesley had a huge apartment in Kendall Square, so big that we each had our own room. He had us living in style, which Natasha loved. He rented cars for us—Natasha even got a red Ferrari for a little while—and got us rooms at the Four Seasons just for a change of scenery. A couple of times Natasha and I went to the mall with one of his credit cards and just shopped and shopped until we were so tired we could barely walk. That's probably where my designer-label habit started. But life was different at Wesley's. Even though we had one more person living with us, we seemed less like a family than ever before. Natasha was going off on her own more and more. Except for the occasional shopping trip, she and I hardly ever hung out by ourselves.

Despite the fact that Natasha liked the way Wesley took care of her, she didn't really care about him. One day, out of the blue, she came home and started to gather up her stuff. "I've met someone," she told me matter-of-factly, "and I'm going to live with him."

"Can I come?" I asked her. She hardly looked at me when she said no.

Kayla was the one who told Wesley that Natasha had left. She knew the guy Natasha had run off with too. He was a drug dealer who lived in Buffalo, and I got the feeling, though she didn't say it directly, that he was not a nice guy. There was something else that Kayla wasn't saying, which was that this dealer hung out with a lot of junkies and that Natasha was becoming one herself. She hadn't just run off with a drug dealer, she'd gotten into drugs, and hard drugs too. She had probably gone off with the guy because he promised her a steady supply, which, in her eyes, beat Wesley's apartment and cars. I knew she used, but I didn't know how bad it was. Looking back, I realize that Kayla and Wesley must have understood that part of the story perfectly, though they didn't talk about it in front of me.

Wesley was so heartbroken that he sent me to go find Natasha and bring her back. Up until that point, the cars had been for Kayla and Natasha only. I knew how to drive a little, but I didn't have a license. Even though what he gave me to drive was just a beat-up old Buick, I was psyched to get my own car.

Wesley said that he would go himself except he thought Natasha would be more likely to listen to me because she loved me. He was right about that, but I think there was another reason. Despite the fact that he had three girls living in his apartment, two of them prostitutes and two of them underage runaways, he was still running his own business, and I doubt he could have afforded to get caught in the kinds of places I had to go to look for Natasha.

I drove all the way to Buffalo by myself, and I still remember how long and dull that trip was. I thought I was never going to make it. When I finally did, I found Natasha at the dealer's house. I wasn't sure how she was going to react to me just showing up, but she acted happy to see me. I asked her to come back with me, and she agreed, just like that.

I still remember how much fun we had driving back together. While the trip up there seemed to take forever, the way back just flew by. We talked about normal stuff, like music, clothes, and boys. We talked about how great it was to be together again and all the places we wanted to go. We talked about how much we loved being free, how much better it was than being stuck in a youth center. When our favorite songs came on the radio, we rolled down the windows and sang out loud together, just like we had done while we hid in the woods after running away. It was like old times, if you can have old times at the age of fifteen or sixteen. But really a lot had changed since then. Still, we never talked about the ugly side of our lives since leaving the youth center, the people who'd wanted to take—and had taken—advantage of us, the drugs that were taking over Natasha, how scary it all was sometimes. We just didn't, but I wished we had.

Our reunion was great, but it was short-lived. It wasn't long before Natasha left us again. She went back to her boyfriend in Buffalo, without saying a word to any of us this time.

Kayla and I stayed with Wesley for a while after Natasha left, but things were never the same. Even though he didn't say it, we both knew we weren't the ones he really cared about, although he didn't kick us out. Strangely, Kayla and Wesley actually got closer after that, and I began to feel like a third wheel. A few years later, Wesley ended up marrying Kayla, and they moved to the country together. It's like a real-life *Pretty Woman* story. I guess for some people that kind of fairy tale can come true after all, but I just knew it wasn't going to happen that way for me. I was nearly sixteen then, Natasha was gone, and it was time for me to get a life of my own.

CHAPTER 5

On My Own

When it came time for me to leave Wesley's house, I moved in with my first real boyfriend (meaning the guy I finally lost my virginity with), Jackson. He lived in Rhode Island but came to Boston to work a lot, which is how I met him. He ran girls, just like Dante and Julio, so he knew everyone that I knew. He'd come around and pay attention to me when everyone else was chatting up Natasha and Kayla. Back then, that was all it took for me to fall for him.

Independence didn't come easy to me, and Jackson wasn't a good way to start things off. He was really fucked up. When he beat me, he'd say things like "If you love someone, that's how you show her. A guy who doesn't do this obviously doesn't care at all."

Jackson was a lot bigger than me and strong. He worked out all the time and had the compactly muscled physique of a boxer, which is no wonder since he loved to hit things. I remember one time when he beat me for hours and hours without stopping while I just watched the seconds tick by on the wall clock. It got to the point where whenever we were in a car together, I would keep my hand on the door handle and imagine jumping out and making a run for it. I would wonder if staying with him was worse than falling out of a moving car. And if I made it, would I find a cop or someone to help me before he could come after me? I never did it because I never thought I would make it. He just seemed so much more powerful than anyone else, I didn't think anyone could possibly have saved me from him. The sickest part was that I really believed he loved me and that I needed him. I couldn't leave him because he was all I had.

I was at Jackson's house in Rhode Island when his brother got caught crossing the border into Canada with two underage girls. The cops picked his brother up, and either someone tipped them off or they could just tell something wasn't right because they began an investigation into his background. That led them to Jackson, which led them to me.

When the police found out who I was, they sent me back to the youth center in Maine, which was when I saw Natasha for the last time. I hadn't been back very long when Natasha came in escorted by a couple of staff. She looked completely broken, pale and sad, with her beautiful long blond hair all tangled and dirty like a rat's nest. When I saw her, I yelled out to her, "Natasha!" She turned and looked at me with dead eyes. She didn't answer, but I don't know if that was because she was too out of it or because the staff was ushering her past without stopping. Maybe it was because she just didn't want to. I hope that wasn't the reason.

They took Natasha straight to the monitored ward, where they check on people every ten to fifteen minutes to make sure they don't commit suicide. She must have been in really bad shape to end up there. When I first saw her, I let myself imagine that life was going to be better after that. She'd get out of the monitored ward eventually, we would pick up where we'd left off, and I wouldn't be alone anymore. But I never even got a chance to talk to her. She ran away as soon as she could. I cried all night when I found out that she was gone.

Even then, I think I still had some hope that things would work out for Natasha and me someday down the road, that she would come back when she was ready and that we'd hang out again like we always did. Now I realize that there was no going back for her at that point. This was the life she'd chosen for herself, and I think she knew what she was getting into. Looking back, I can see that Natasha was always drawn to that life like a moth to flame: the way she was fascinated by Julio in the beginning, the way she wanted to become a prostitute and pushed Dante to let her, the way she used to stare at working girls on the street, even the ones that most of us choose not to look at. It seems like it was her destiny. Or maybe it's just the life she thought she deserved; I may be the only person who believes she didn't.

Natasha did her best to protect me. She always found a place for us to stay. If someone wanted to take advantage of me, she'd offer up herself instead. And before she took off, she made sure I was somewhere safe. Wesley may not have been the ideal caretaker, but he probably never would have kicked me out, and he wasn't dangerous. I don't think it was an accident that Natasha set up that situation before taking off on her own. I easily could have become a prostitute too, with some pimp feeding me drugs and telling me what to do, or out on the street fending for myself. But I didn't, and I know how lucky I am. Believe me, I know. And I have Natasha to thank for getting me through my most vulnerable years relatively intact.

I think Natasha's dead now. If not from the drugs, then from something else just as bad. I found out a few years later that Julio, as well as one of his girls, had died of AIDS, and I'm almost certain that Natasha slept with him at least once. I also heard that Natasha was working in a really bad place that was full of dirty junkies. Any number of things could have finally put an end to Natasha, but whatever it was, I'm afraid it was painful and ugly. A lot of people probably wouldn't think so, but I know she deserved a whole lot better than what she got.

It wasn't long after Natasha ran away from the youth center that I did the same. I had always hated living in those places, but after having tasted freedom for so long, my last stint was unbearable. The place was basically like kid jail. Because I had previously run away, I couldn't stay in the big, dormitory-style house I'd stayed in before. Instead, they put me in another building where I had to spend most of my time in a cubicle-size room with a lock on the door and nothing in it but a narrow bed. There was no need for anything else, since I wasn't allowed to have any stuff. All the kids wore green uniforms, except for the ones, like me, who had tried to escape; we wore orange ones to make us easier to spot. Even the time we were allowed out of our rooms was strictly controlled. There was a TV, but we had to watch what the staff chose for us. We could play cards or write letters, but that got boring quickly. Besides, who was I going to write letters to? I remember spending hours at a time in my room, just pacing back and forth to get some exercise. I probably looked like a caged animal. I know I felt like one.

Now part of me wishes I had stayed rather than gone back to Jackson, which is what I did. But the way I thought about things back then, being at that youth center was the worst thing that could have happened to me. I had lost my best friend, and Jackson was the only person who even cared that I existed. It was inevitable that I would escape as soon as I got the chance.

That was my last time at that or any youth center. I managed to keep a low enough profile until I turned eighteen that I was never sent back again. Actually, what happened was that I got better at lying, so when I did get picked up for something, usually for fighting or underage drinking or reckless driving or too many parking tickets, the cops couldn't connect me to that place in Maine because I wouldn't tell them my real name or where I came from. I have Julio to thank for helping me develop those skills. I was scared the first couple of times the cops picked me up, but pretty soon I realized how easy it was to deal with them. I even came up with my own Rolodex of fake names to make it more fun. I often called myself Angel, which I thought was funny because I knew I wasn't one, or Roxanne after the Police song. For my last name, I'd choose one of the few Korean words I still remembered. One of my favorites was Halmuni, which means "grandmother." Angel Grandmother. The cops could usually tell I was bullshitting them, but they didn't care. I was never picked up for anything big enough for them to give a shit. I'd always picture some Korean cop getting ahold of my arrest report and having a good laugh when he read it. That trick worked for me for years. It would probably still work except that now I actively try *not* to get arrested.

To make my own money while I was living with Jackson (because there was no way he was going to give me much to spend) I danced at strip clubs in and around Boston. At one of the nicer spots, I met Andre. He was so smooth, I couldn't help but notice him as soon as he walked in the place. He drove a white Cadillac and always wore nice clothes, mostly custom-made suits that hung just right off his six-foot-one frame, with matching gators in every color. He was always draped in huge, expensive diamonds and either a mink coat or a fox bomber jacket when it was cold. He was tall, dark, and handsome, with dark eyes, dark skin, and dark hair, which made him stand out among all the losers who frequented the place. But he also stood out because he seemed mature, like he had his shit together. He was in his early thirties, and he knew how to talk to women. Most of the guys who came into the club made me feel like I was working hard for my money. They were drunk, rude idiots, for the most part, but not Andre. When he came around, all the girls were happy to shower him with lots of attention.

One day I was dancing near where he was sitting when I over-heard him pick up on one of my co-workers. My ears perked up when I heard him rattle off the digits of his phone number, and I repeated them over and over in my head until I could find a time to sneak off and write them down. I didn't really plan to call him, but I just knew that I wanted his number for some reason.

From then on, not only was Andre on my radar screen but I was on his. He came in often enough to notice that I regularly had black eyes and bruises. You can't hide much when you're stripping, but sometimes I'd keep my sunglasses on while I danced. I was hoping that the guys, if they thought about it at all, would assume that they were just a cool prop or that I had a hangover, but they were really a dead giveaway that I was hiding something. Andre always knew what was going on. He pulled me aside one day, looked through the lenses into my eyes, and said, "You don't need that." He didn't say what he was referring to, but I knew. Back then no one was telling me things like that.

Jackson was the kind of guy who was always mad at the world, and he liked to take it out on me. To be fair, he had some good reasons to be upset. Not long before I met him, the love of his life, Rachel, had been abducted, taken to a warehouse, hung on a rope, and sodomized with various objects before being murdered and left to rot. Her naked, decomposing body wasn't found until some time after the fact. The police didn't know who did it then, and the whole thing had left Jackson a little crazy in the head. I don't know if he had been a nice guy before that happened or not—my guess is that he had always been an asshole—but I do know that it haunted him.

Later I found out that the guy who murdered Rachel was actually Joel Rifkin, one of the country's most notorious serial killers. I was in a holding cell in New York—long after I'd left Jackson—when they caught him. (I was there because I had been picked up during a routine bust of the Asian "massage parlor" I was running.) I was sitting on the floor of central booking playing spades with some other girls when I looked up at the television set, which was tuned to the local news. They were showing this video of the police chasing a truck on the interstate. The police had tried to pull this guy over for not having a license plate, but he didn't know that was all they wanted, so he tried to run. The chase ended with him running into a pole, after which they found the body of a dead prostitute in the bed of his truck.

I was laughing at the stupidity of this guy when they flashed a picture of his face. It was Joel Rifkin, and I recognized him instantly. He'd come into one of the clubs I had worked at several times. I'd even danced for him myself once or twice. He was the kind of guy who was often looking for girls for hire, and that was the scary part. I knew for a fact that he had kept company with working girls lots of times and nothing bad had happened to them. Most of the time he acted like any other customer, so no one had any idea that we should be afraid of him. Sometimes people just snap without warning, I guess, but that made the whole thing even harder to wrap my head around. When I saw his face, I just kept repeating out loud, over and over again to no one in particular, "I know that guy. I know that guy." I think I must have been in shock. My whole body went cold, and I vowed never to watch the news again. To this day, I never have.

Later I found out that Rifkin preyed on ethnic women who worked in the sex industry and that he scouted for his victims at strip clubs in and around big cities like Boston and New York. That was why I knew several people who had had contact with him. It was freaky. I don't know why he targeted that type, but he obviously had some serious issues. A friend told me that he killed another girl I knew, a beautiful Spanish hooker named Venus. She was five months pregnant when he got her, and he cut out her baby and left the two bodies in two different Dumpsters in Central Park. I don't go to Central Park anymore either.

What happened to Jackson's girlfriend was the kind of thing that people just never get over. Eventually, I started to understand that and realized that if Jackson couldn't get over it, then he probably wasn't going to change. The idea that he might always be the way he was frightened me more than the beatings themselves. One night, for no reason at all, he lost it on me so bad that I had to run into the bathroom and lock the door to protect myself.

All I had on that night was my pajamas, with eleven dollars in the pocket for some reason, and a pair of socks. Still, I decided it would be better to crawl out the window than to face Jackson. There I was, all by myself with barely anything on, and the only thing I could think to do was call Andre. I had memorized his number, so I went to find a pay phone and called him. Luckily he answered and didn't hang up when I started crying hysterically. He just asked me what was wrong. When I told him, he said, "Stay there. I'm sending someone to pick you up."

Andre brought me to the apartment of one of his "girls," at least that's who he told me she was. Later I found out she was his wife. She instantly saw me as competition and wasn't very nice to me when she found out I'd be staying for a while. Andre told her to find me some clothes to wear, and she returned with the most hideous outfits, which made me look awful. Andre bought her a diamond ring to smooth things over, but it didn't really work. She hated having me there, and it showed. Pretty soon Andre came to get me and took me to a new place. It was a two-bedroom condo in a gated community outside of Boston. It was big and beautiful, and I felt safe there. It was our new home.

Andre became my whole world after that. When I moved in with him, I realized I didn't know anything. I mean, really nothing. I'd been on my own, off and on, for a couple of years at that point, but still, I was pathetic. Andre took me in, but more important, he taught me how to live. He started with the basics, showing me how to make myself breakfast and, as long as I was at it, how to make some for him too. He showed me how to clean up after myself, how to take care of myself, and eventually, he showed me how to cook more complicated things than toast and cereal. Every man needs a strong woman behind him, and every player needs a wife. I fulfilled that role for him. I knew instinctively that he was going to mold me into the perfect girl, and I was the perfect age for him to do so.

Andre knew how to do a lot of things. He was an all-around businessman. He ran a few girls, and he owned a few aboveboard businesses, like a barbershop in Boston, but the way he made most of his cash was by dealing drugs. He was real good with money, so after I had mastered the art of a clean kitchen, he started to teach me basic economics.

The other thing that Andre taught me about was respect. I didn't have any at the time, but if I was going to survive, he told me I needed to learn how to get some. If it hadn't been for Andre showing me how, who knows where I'd be today.

In the world we lived in, there were really only two ways to gain respect. The first was money: people respect you if you have cash to spend. When we'd go out, Andre always made a show of spending lots of money. The clothes he wore, the cars he drove, the liquor he drank—it was always intentionally expensive and everyone noticed. And it was the same for me. I became his prize, so I had to look good. I got leather and suede pants, gator boots, and after thirty days of being together, a gorgeous full-length mink coat with a fox lining; after sixty days together, I got a rock for my finger worth thousands.

The second way to gain respect was through violence: people respect you if they fear you. Andre most often chose to gain respect by spending money, but violence—or the threat of violence—was really a more effective way, and he knew just when and how to use that method too. Andre wasn't afraid of using violence to get what he wanted; people knew not to mess with him, and pretty soon, they learned that he wouldn't tolerate them messing with me either. One night when we were out with his friends, I was complaining about something and one of his acquaintances called me a bitch. Andre gave the guy an icy stare.

"You got that backwards," he said calmly and quietly. "You're the bitch."

Andre then whispered something to the guy next to him, who

nodded and immediately left us. Meanwhile, the guy who'd called me a bitch tried to explain himself, giving reasons for saying what he said. As if that made any difference.

Pretty soon Andre's partner (back then he called all his side-kicks "partners") came back with a can of dog food and handed it to him.

"Now who's the bitch?" Andre asked, pulling back the tab on the can and holding it out toward the guy who had disrespected me.

It was obvious to all of us that Andre wouldn't hesitate to hurt this guy if he didn't do what Andre was asking. The guy knew if he didn't take that can of dog food, he probably wouldn't make it home in one piece that night. He looked at me for just a moment before he took the can. Andre made him get down on his hands and knees and eat out of the can right in front of us. After that, Andre just ignored him, like he never even existed. That guy never spoke to me again. I knew then just how powerful it can really be to let everyone know you're not afraid of a little violence.

In fact, Andre earned respect in a third, unusual way, which was just by being a straight-up guy. He never talked about it, but I know people respected him because he wasn't a bullshitter. If he told you the drugs he was selling you were going to be a certain price, then that was the price they would be. He didn't change the deal on you at the last minute or take advantage of you just because he could if he wanted to. He was no petty thief. He was too big for that, and as a result people respected him even more. What's more, they wanted to deal with him.

Andre was the one who set me up in my very first business. My partner was Suzie, a Thai woman who was the cutest little thing you've ever seen. She was older than me but looked really young. She must have been about twenty-one, because she always got served at the bars and clubs we went to. But then again, maybe not. She didn't look a day over eighteen, and no bartender would ever card a girl that adorable.

Andre and I used to travel back and forth between Boston and New York City all the time back then. Andre would say it was "for business," but I didn't really know what his business was in the beginning. All I knew was that every time we went to New York, we had the best time. We'd eat in great restaurants all over the city and hang out with cool people who dressed just like Andre. He hung out with a group of rappers, and we'd go to their concerts and video shoots and drink bottles of Dom P that were always on ice in the backs of their big cars. Andre would dress me in furs and drape me in diamonds to take me to clubs where we'd sit at private tables like superstars. I was tiny compared with him—a full ten inches shorter and still rail thin—but we dressed to match and made quite an impression whenever we walked into a room together.

The first time I met Suzie she tried to pick me up. She just walked up to me in one of the New York clubs, this tiny girl with spiky black hair who was totally butch yet feminine and sweet-looking at the same time. She had all the confidence in the world, so naturally I liked her right away. Hooking up wasn't going to happen—I was very attached to Andre, and besides, I'm not gay—so instead we decided to become business partners. I was about seventeen.

Suzie was from Thailand, but she had married a powerful businessman, a founder and owner of a major Japanese corporation, when she was thirteen. The marriage had been arranged by her parents, and she was his fifth wife. Naturally she hated him and got away from him as soon as she could. I always thought one of the reasons she became a lesbian was that she hated him so much. I never knew exactly how she got away or why he didn't come after her. Maybe he did, but she never seemed to be afraid that he'd catch up to her.

Andre was always looking for new business opportunities, and he wanted to find something for me to do with myself. I was so young and thought he was the best thing in the whole world. I doted on him, followed him around, and generally annoyed the hell out of him. He was a decent guy, so he would never throw me out or tell me to just get lost—he cared about me, and besides, where would I go? But he was feeling crowded and thought I needed a project, something to keep me busy and out of his hair. So when Suzie came up with the idea, he gave me the money to start up a brothel with her.

By that time we were living in Fort Lee, New Jersey, and I had worked my way up to being Andre's personal money manager. I had also learned a lot about the drug business he was involved in and how it worked. I stacked his bills, and once a month, I gathered up those stacks and took them to a bank thirty miles away for deposit in his safety deposit box. Andre was the one who taught me that $10,000 worth of $100 bills fit perfectly into a small Ziploc sandwich bag, which is a trick I still use to this day to keep track of the cash I have on hand. He also showed me that people like us could store money safely in the bank as long as it was in a safety deposit box and not an account. He even bought me a Cadillac Coupe when I was seventeen so that I could do my errands. I also danced at a strip club called The Body Shop on 123rd and Lexington in Harlem, but Andre was right, even with the dancing and the job I did for him, I still had too much time on my hands.

Suzie and I rented an entire floor of a commercial building on West Twenty-first Street in Manhattan to use as our brothel. It was just this large, open warehouse space when we got it, so we had contractors come in to transform it into something workable. We had walls put up to form six booths with doors, each of which was just big enough for a twin mattress set on an elevated platform, a chair in the corner for clothes, and a narrow walkway. It was just the basics—white walls, no decoration, no frills. There was also a big wash area with showers on one side for the girls and wash beds on the other for the customers.

When a client walked into our place, he'd pay an entrance fee of $40 to $60, which bought him a massage on one of those wash beds. The girls would sit on benches that lined the perimeter of the entry room and cop their most seductive or demure poses when a customer walked in. He'd pick out the girl he wanted, and then they'd head for the wash area. If he wanted to continue on to one of the booths after that, he'd have to negotiate with the girl directly. Generally speaking, a $120 "tip" would get a guy a hand job, and an extra $200 would get him sex. Those girls knew how to negotiate too, even with the businessmen who were our most frequent type of customer, though we really attracted all types of men.

We placed ads in the backs of magazines like *Girls* and *Screw* and newspapers like *The Village Voice* to draw customers. Those ads, which featured pictures of young Asian girls, also attracted women looking for work. We weren't all that picky about who we hired, and we would try out just about any decent-looking woman who came by. All kinds ended up working for us; it wasn't just the young, poor, and helpless. Most of them were either Thai or Korean, and one of our biggest moneymakers was actually a sixty-year-old Korean woman. She wasn't ashamed to tell us her age because she looked like she was about thirty and had no trouble attracting men. She had had work done on just about every part of her body.

One of my favorite ladies was a woman who became a really good girlfriend of mine. She was Chinese and in her twenties, but she looked nineteen at most. Her name was Carole, and she had grown up in Chinatown with nine older brothers, all of them gang members. Her brothers looked out for her by controlling almost every aspect of her life. She was never allowed to date when she was growing up, so she got married really young, to escape her brothers' care, I guess, although we never talked about why. Why just wasn't a question that any of us asked about anything. "Why are we here?" "Why are we doing this?" If anyone wondered about these things, they never brought them up. Things just were the way they were and that was that.

Carole hated her husband. She would say things like "Ugh. It's Tuesday. I've got to go home and fuck my husband," like it was laundry day or something. She was hysterical like that. She was very innocent looking, almost like a little girl, but you never knew what was going to come out of her mouth. Carole worked only once in a while, and when she did, she would do maybe one or two customers and then go home. She didn't actually like sex very much. She was so small, she said it hurt her.

Carole never said why she came to us. Maybe it was her way of getting back at her husband or her brothers or all the men in her life. She didn't seem like she needed the money. Maybe she just wanted somewhere to go where people would accept her. Separate from the work area was a private area with a kitchen and a girls-only lounge. When they weren't working, the women would play cards and other games, eat meals together, or just sit around drinking tea and gossiping. From the beginning, the house was a place where ladies would gather and just hang out.

When I noticed how people liked to hang out at the brothel, I came up with another way to make money. As I said, I think I am kind of a born entrepreneur because I was always thinking about things like that. When I had nothing better to do, I often found myself at underground bars playing the gambling machines (the beginning of a little problem that would get me into some big trouble later on). I knew how much money I had lost to those machines, so I had a couple brought in for the girls to play while they waited for clients or for the clients to play while they waited for girls. They were a hit and eventually even became a bad habit for some of the girls, who never wanted to stop playing them.

As it turned out, there wasn't much work for me to do because the place really ran itself. There would be about fifteen girls working at one time, and some of the girls actually lived there. They'd use the booths as their bedrooms when no one was working in them. Other than our initial construction costs, we didn't have much overhead. We hired security guards, one who worked during the day and two who came at night, so we could be open twenty-four hours a day. The bulk of our business happened at night, however, so, as far as I know, none of the neighbors in our building, which were all day businesses—fabric warehouses and that kind of thing—knew what was going on. Or if they did, they never bothered us.

The business did do what Andre had hoped it would—it gave me somewhere to go and something to do whenever I needed it (or he needed it). I liked to gamble and talk with the ladies, so I spent a lot of time there. Everyone was older than me, and in the Asian cultures that most of the ladies came from, younger women have to do what the older ones say. That's just the way things work. So even though I was supposed to be their boss, the ladies were always telling me what to do and sending me out to get them cigarettes or buy them nail polish. They kept me busy, and I always did what they asked.

The Mamasan, especially, always looked to me if she needed help with her work. She was in her fifties, and her job was to take care of all the girls, clean the house, and cook for them. We often called her "*ojama*," which is the Korean word for "caretaker." She lived there too. When the place was finally busted by the cops, she was the only one they didn't take to jail. She just kept saying "Me Mamasan" over and over and over again, and the cops knew what she meant. Every place like ours had its own Mamasan, a kind of den mother, an older woman who took care of the place, and the police usually took pity on them. If they knew how much money these ladies made, though, they might not have been so generous. Our Mamasan was paid by the girls. Each one gave her $250 a week in what was called "pock-up money," some of which went toward basic living expenses but most of which she would send back home to her family in Korea. With an average of fifteen girls working at once, well, you do the math.

We were open for about four months when the cops finally came. I'm not sure how they found us exactly, but no one was particularly surprised or scared when they did. Like I said, we advertised in major media sources, so it's not like we were hard to find. That's just the way things worked then. The brothel business was a game of how long can you keep things going before you get caught. It was like gambling in that way. The cops came through the house and arrested everyone inside except the Mamasan, me included. They took us down to the station and booked us, but they didn't really care about our business. They just wanted their arrest record to look good. (Remember, that was the Giuliani era.) So the next morning, after they had filed their reports and tallied the number of arrests, they let everyone go. And none of us had even given them our real names.

If they had known I was one of the owners of the house, the cops would have been much harder on me. But I pretended to be one of the working girls who could "speaky no English." After all, I was Asian, like most of them were, and just a teenager. Of course the cops believed me and let me go the next morning along with everyone else. Suzie and I both practically looked like kids and each weighed barely more than a hundred pounds. No one would ever suspect that a couple of girls like us were in charge of such a place. Most people still have a hard time believing things like that.

CHAPTER 6

Baltimore or Less

Andre may have been a straight-up guy when it came to business, but he didn't live by the same standards when it came to relationships. He left me alone so often and was so unwilling to tell me where he was going or where he'd been, that I began to think he was cheating on me. Of course, he wouldn't even have considered it cheating. I was expected to be faithful, but for a hustler like him, the same rule never applies. Regardless, I still felt betrayed or, at least, neglected, so I decided to beat him at his own game. One time when we were "taking time apart" (which meant he was off with some other woman), I started up with a hot Chippendales dancer I met when my Thai friends and I went to a show. (I've had a big thing for dancers ever since.) The whole point of the dancer was to get back at Andre, but he didn't even notice. He was too busy traveling to California, where, I later found out, his other girlfriend, the mother of a child pop star, lived.

I finally found out for certain about the other woman because he eventually took me to California. He said we were going "on vacation," but once we got there, he left me alone in the hotel room the entire time. When I did see him and he admitted to me where he'd been and who he'd been with, I was furious. I was sure she wasn't the only woman he'd been screwing around with, but with her it was even worse. It wasn't just sex with this woman, the two of them had a real relationship.

Just before our trip to California I had found out I was pregnant. I hadn't told Andre yet because of my suspicions about the other woman, and after they were confirmed, I vowed he would never know. I hopped a plane back home and, soon after, packed a bag and got on a train. I didn't really care where I was going as long as it was away from there. I was running away again, but part of me was excited about it. I used to love taking the train back then. I racked up so many Amtrak miles during that period of my life, I probably should have bought stock in the company.

I ended up in Baltimore. I didn't have a plan for what to do when I got there, so I went to a shelter to spend the night. Because I looked so young, the people who worked there started asking questions. I told them that I was pregnant and that I had just left my boyfriend, thinking that would be a good enough explanation. Instead, it brought on more questions. They asked me if he had abused me, and I told them the truth, that he hit me sometimes.

Andre had a strict business policy of not sampling the merchandise, but he never could stick to that. He was a good guy most of the time, but he had also been a heroin addict before I met him. He didn't like being that way, and he tried his best to get off it. He did for a while, but then I'd see him going back down the wrong path, which usually started with just some pot, which led to more things, and eventually led to smoking crack. He went back and forth and back and forth like that for years. For most of our relationship, I thought I was going to marry him one day, but I also knew full well that there were two sides to my Gemini, the side that had rescued me from a bad situation and taught me how to take care of myself, and the drug side. The drug side was not pretty, and he would often lose his temper with me when he was in one of his hazes.

When I got to the shelter, I was so pissed at Andre that I wasn't thinking too much about his good side. I'm sure I painted a pretty bad picture of him when I described our relationship to the people there. I don't know why I was so honest with them—it really isn't my habit to be honest with strangers about myself or my personal life—but maybe it was my preservation instinct that made me do it. Every truthful word I spoke to them seemed to drive Andre further and further away from me, like the more I admitted about our relationship, the harder it would be for me to go back to him. At the time, if you had asked me why I left Andre, I would have said it was because of jealousy, because of the other woman, or women. But now I wonder if some part of me wanted out for other reasons. Andre was always going to be the one with the power in a relationship, there was no question about that, and the only way to see if I could get some power of my own would be to get away from him. Even then I knew I didn't want someone to have power over me for the rest of my life, not even if it was someone I loved.

Pretty soon I was gathering up my things so the people at the shelter could take me somewhere else. Because I was young and pregnant, they placed me in a battered women's shelter instead of the homeless shelter I'd gone to. I didn't think of myself as a "battered woman," but I think they got the idea that I was running away from Andre because he was dangerous, not because of his wandering dick. I didn't care what they thought. The sympathy was kind of nice, and it gave me somewhere to go. The regular shelter was a freak show anyway, so I was happy to be moved to a new place. At least the battered women's shelter was cleaner and safer.

It was the second shelter that arranged for my abortion. I wasn't going back to Andre and I couldn't take care of a kid by myself, that much I knew. I had no place to live, no money, no work. I don't remember there being much of a moral debate about it. I guess everyone, including me, thought it was the most logical thing to do.

I did see Andre again after that, when I went back to New York for a visit. When I told him about the abortion, he cried. He was a very religious guy, a regular churchgoer who'd come from a strong Catholic family and whose mother still had a big influence in his life. He said he would have wanted to have it and he would have married me if he'd known. Too little too late. He even tried to weasel his way back into my life after that, but I was done with him.

I still keep in touch with Andre and even see him now and then. I feel like I owe him a lot. He took care of me and taught me things at a time when I didn't know much of anything at all. Andre, despite all his faults and the way things ended, was my first true love. I know I wouldn't be where I am today without him, so I still think the world of him.

Some years later, when I was visiting Boston, I went by his uncle's beauty parlor and left a message for Andre with my phone number. I was at Foxwoods gambling when I got his call. He drove all the way up there to see me again, and we had a great reunion. I realized then that I had meant a lot to him too. I remember one night years ago when the two of us were living together and some dope boys broke down our door to rob us. We were in bed, and I immediately jumped on top of him while he was sleeping and covered his face with my body. I just kept yelling at the guys over and over again, "We're not looking, take whatever you want, we're not looking!" They did just that. I know that if I hadn't done what I did, Andre would have sprung out of bed and confronted them, probably getting us killed in the process. Realizing that I had saved his life, he got down on one knee afterward and begged me to stay with him forever. An act that humble was totally out of character for someone as proud and strong as Andre, and I knew it. It really meant something.

Andre may have wanted me to be his wife, but he also didn't ever want to really settle down. Still, he was always honest with me, even about that. Ruthless but honest. His philosophy was that, if he knew something would upset me, he just wouldn't tell me about it, and if he didn't explain, there was no deception. That's a philosophy I still believe in to this day. I'm not a liar, but I do believe that my business is my business and no one else's. And in all the ways that I admired him, I *am* Andre now. We are both cold and honest, but when we love, we love deeply.

After the abortion, I got out of that women's shelter as fast as I could. That place was just too depressing. The women there were like ghosts. Most of them had come from really bad places and would wander around with vacant stares like they'd had the life knocked out of them. I couldn't take it. The shelter tried to hook me up with a job, some minimum-wage, by-the-hour thing, but I had other ideas in mind.

I knew I needed to start up some sort of business, something that could support me so I didn't have to rely on another guy, but I didn't know what to do. This was the first time I'd be starting something completely on my own, but I was sure that I could figure it out.

Since the brothel business had done pretty well in New York, I thought I would try the same thing in Baltimore. I started out by doing some research into the local market. I began by simply pulling out the yellow pages, turning to the "Escort" section, and making some calls.

My method was simple. I would pretend I was looking for a job, and then I would use that cover to ask a lot of questions about how their businesses worked. I had a young voice and told them (honestly) that I was Asian and not yet twenty. They were all happy to talk to me. No one thought for even a moment that I might be a threat or competition. Why would they?

One of the agencies even hooked me up with a girl who worked for them. They thought she might be better able to answer my questions. Her name was Maya, and when we met, we hit it off immediately. After we talked for a while at her agency's office, she offered me more than just info; she invited me to come along on one of her appointments.

What I learned from her was that I could have set up a brothel like I'd had in New York, but it would have been dangerous and there was a much easier and safer way of doing business in Baltimore. The industry was very different there. When I went on the call with Maya, we showed up at the customer's door together and Maya explained to him that I was "in training." The guy was a bit surprised, but I think he thought he was getting a bonus. Maya collected the money up-front, as working girls always do, and then asked him what he wanted to do for the next hour. He blushed, mumbled something about a blow job, and then looked stunned when Maya corrected him. "Oh no, we can't do that. We're just escorts, not hookers." When the guy finally understood that he'd been fooled and wasn't going to get what he wanted, he let us go early.

That was how a lot of businesses worked all over town. My research showed that most of the agencies listed in the yellow pages were either real, legitimate escort agencies (the kind that advertise girls for "companionship only") or what I call "rip-off agencies." This meant that the girls who worked for them were actually just companions as well, but because of the way they were marketed, none of the customers knew it until it was too late.

The ads for the rip-off agencies were full of innuendo but no promises. They offered "Foxy Playmates for All Occasions," "Party Girls in Half an Hour," and sometimes even "Full Body Massage!!!" Some kept it simple, saying something like "Serving the Baltimore Area" next to a picture of a sultry young girl. But the clients knew what they meant, or at least they thought they did. A guy would call up to make an appointment expecting full service, but then a girl would show up at his hotel room or wherever, collect her money, and ask, just like Maya did, "So, what do you want to do now?"

That question would cause most guys to stammer, because you don't usually have to tell a real working girl what to do next. Some would think it was a sting operation and wonder if they were being recorded. If they actually got around to asking for sex, the girl would say something like "I'm sorry, but that's illegal and I can't do anything illegal." Then she would say, "I could give you a body rub for an additional hundred-dollar tip but not a real massage. I'm not licensed to give massages." There was never any actual sex involved.

You'd think that it would be a dangerous game, that guys would get really pissed off about being scammed and girls would get hurt as a result, but the girls were really good at getting in and out quickly, at keeping calm and being matter-of-fact about the whole situation, at putting the guys on the defensive for assuming they were prostitutes. Most of the guys, who were usually just your average businessmen, were embarrassed by the whole thing and would either take the "body rub" or just send the girl home. A few would try to negotiate for a "happy ending," but it rarely happened. If a guy did get angry, which they obviously did sometimes, the girl would just call the cops. After all, she hadn't technically done anything wrong.

Of course that kind of setup only works on a guy once, so the majority of customers had to be out-of-towners. Still, there always seemed to be people coming and going through Baltimore on business, so I found out that it worked again and again and again. There were even some customers who didn't want anything more than company. They were the best ones. Those were often the drug users, who just wanted someone to be with them while they did what they did. Maya had one repeat customer, an importer from down south, who hired her for forty-eight straight hours one time at her hourly rate of $200. He didn't even try to make a deal, so obviously she banked off him. He was a wealthy man who just wanted someone to lie next to him and hold his hand while he tried to fall asleep after having drunk himself into oblivion. She thought he probably had nightmares based on the way he tossed and turned and the noises he made while he slept. But during the day he'd take her shopping and out to eat. She thought he was a pretty cool guy who just wanted a drinking partner until he got really fucked up one night and started ranting about how the aliens were coming.

When it came time for me to open up my own shop, I did as those around me did ("When in Rome" and all that) and opened a "rip-off agency." I didn't need as much start-up cash as I had needed in New York because there was no space to rent, no construction costs, no security guys to hire, which was perfect since I was on my own. I just needed enough money to place a few ads and a couple of girls (most of whom I stole from the agencies that had been so open with me) to visit clients. Just like that, I was open for business.

Naturally, I had a lot of unhappy customers calling me, but they were no trouble at all when they heard my routine response: "What you are asking for is illegal, sir. We are an upscale escort agency that offers companionship only. The young lady is there to keep you company, and frankly, all this discussion is cutting into your quality time with her, which you've already paid for. Unfortunately, we can't offer you a refund or a discount because she has done her best to provide you with exceptional service. If you are going to turn this into a situation, sir, we will have no choice but to call the police."

As long as I was polite and kept my voice level, that speech usually put an end to a difficult situation, but not always. Maya, who was one of the first girls to come to work for me, once had a congressman for a customer who freaked out so much that she had to call the cops. Even after they arrived, this guy continued to rant about how he had "paid for S-E-X!" and hadn't gotten what he'd been promised. That kind of talk quickly landed him in jail. He was such an idiot. This was around the time of the scandal with Dick Morris, the political consultant for Bill Clinton who had to resign after he got caught—pictures and all—with a hooker. The media were focusing on that type of story back then, and after the congressman incident, Maya and I got a call from the *Sally Jessy Raphael* show. We thought it might be fun to go on TV and spill the beans about our industry, so we told the producer that we'd do it.

It always seems to come as a shock to the public when famous men get caught with hookers, which makes me laugh. I knew one girl who was hired several times by a very well-known, very gorgeous movie star. (He was so good-looking that she even began stalking him after he stopped calling her.) Someone like that can obviously get a girl without paying her. Besides, he has so much to lose, why would he risk it? People outside the industry ask me questions like that all the time—why do guys take such stupid risks?—especially if the famous guys in question are married. The truth is, if these guys wanted to fuck the same girl time and time again, they'd just get mistresses. But that's not what they want. There are a lot reasons why guys do what they do, but the point for many of them is that they just want to be around someone who isn't going to judge them for a little while. They have high-stress jobs and they lead complicated lives. Sometimes they just want something uncomplicated, where the outcome is practically assured. Some guys aren't getting it at home, or they're too preoccupied with their work to form real relationships, or they're sex addicts, but many of them actually have pretty good marriages and pretty happy lives. It often isn't about their wives at all; it's about them, about taking a break from their commitments, releasing some stress, and doing exactly what they want to with no consequences, even if it's just for an hour.

I don't really have many well-known clients today, mostly because my service is in New Jersey, where there are plenty of rich but not so many famous men. And that's probably a good thing, since actors, politicians, and other high-profile types can bring with them too much unwanted attention. Maya and I were at the airport with tickets in hand when we changed our minds about the *Sally Jessy Raphael* show. The amount of money we'd been promised just didn't seem worth the effort and potential loss of future business, so we turned around and went home.

I definitely honed my customer-service skills during my Baltimore days. Today, I feel like I can smooth-talk practically any client, no matter what his problem might be, as long as I stay calm. I know exactly what to say in any given situation, but the staying calm part is what I sometimes have trouble with, and it's getting harder. The longer I do this, the shorter my temper. I hear the same damn excuses again and again, from both clients and girls, and I get tired of pretending to care. Patience is a lot more work than it sounds like.

Back then all I really cared about was making money, so I didn't mind all the bullshit as much. It would still be several years before I would learn how to run a business that has all the elements—safety, stability, good money—at once *and* one that provides a great service that clients actually value. The business I have now is rewarding both financially and personally. Who knew you could have that in this industry?

At the time, I was happy with my rip-off agency. As Maya and I spent more time together, we became even better friends. She was a beautiful girl and such a moneymaker. She was also dating a guy who was a top dog in one of the local gangs, and they were the ones who introduced me to my next boyfriend.

Andre had been a powerful guy, but he was nothing compared to Maya's boyfriend, Tito. Tito was tall and lean like a basketball player, but, even if he didn't exactly look like one, he was a real gangster. He asserted his dominance over people every chance he got. He was always arguing with some guy or flirting with some girl just because. His business was drugs too, but if they worked

the same area, Tito probably would have been the guy who provided Andre with the product he sold. Not only was he a bigger
fish, he was one of the top guys in one of the largest drug rings in
the area. He had a whole gang of dealers and runners working for
him. Of course, I found all of this irresistible.

Tito's buddy Allen was a dope boy too, but he worked independ-
ently. He liked to run his own ship; he respected the gangs that controlled most of the city's trade, but he kept himself separate from
them. He believed it was safer and cleaner that way, and I liked that
about him. Plus, he was a fly-looking boy, which was fine by me.
He may have existed under the radar when it came to business, but
in his personal life he was hard to miss. He was nearly six feet tall,
with a muscled, 220-pound frame, and he wore the full-on gear of
a race-car driver during the day. In fact, he was obsessed with anything on wheels. He owned a whole fleet of cars—his most prized
ones being a limited-edition RX-7 and a showroom model Toyota
Supra with a twin turbo engine—many of which he had souped up
just the way he liked them, as lowrides with purple backup lights
and that kind of thing. He even had one of the very first voice-
activated computers installed in his Supra. At night he practically
always wore Versace from head to toe. He was much trendier than
Andre, whose style I'd describe as "old school," but they were both
hard to miss when they went out on the town.

Allen also liked to be in control of everything. Not just business,
but *everything*. He would even tell me that I was not allowed to go
to any of the black clubs in Baltimore, which was ridiculous since
he was black himself. Actually, he was only a quarter black, mixed
with a quarter white and half Hispanic, and it showed in his light
skin, but he called himself "black." Still, he thought the black
clubs were too "ghetto," and no girlfriend of his was going to be
seen in any ghetto places. "You're too good for that," he'd say. For
me it was white-people places or stay home.

But my friend Maya would go *only* to the black clubs because she hated white people and because all the white-people clubs in Baltimore totally sucked. "White people are the ones who are responsible for every dirty, wrong thing in this world," she'd say. "They're the ones who start wars, who oppress people. And it's always the white guys who call up looking to pay some poor girl to do something disgusting. Like golden showers. White men invented those. No self-respecting black man would ever get off on being peed on."

I loved that girl. She was a trip. The funny thing is, Maya also barely looked black, even though she was. Because her skin was a very light brown, she looked Arabic or like a really light-skinned Puerto Rican. Still, she had her rules and Allen had his and I was caught in the middle because I wanted to be around both of them.

Once I tried to sneak into one of Maya's favorite clubs so she and I could hang out. We'd just gotten there when this famous basketball player saw her across the room and came straight over to try to pick her up. She always had that effect on guys everywhere she went. I had no idea who he was, but he had a pick in his nappy hair and was so ballsy about the way he talked to her that I thought he was a whack job. So did Maya. After she turned him down, a friend of ours came over and said, "Do you know who that is?" As soon as she heard who he was, Maya saw dollar signs. She immediately went back over and started sweet-talking him. She really knew how to work people. We were having a great time until Allen showed up. Someone he knew must have seen me and called him to tell him I was there. He knew people everywhere we went.

Allen didn't say a word. He just walked right over to me, picked me up, threw me over his shoulder, and walked out the door. I was screaming for him to put me down and banging on his back with my fists. He barely even noticed. He walked me right past a cop who knew who he was. The cop asked if *he* needed any help, not if I did. Allen said no, threw me in the passenger seat of his car, and drove me home.

It pissed me off when Allen did things like that to me, but at the same time, I understood why he had to keep a firm grip on things all the time. A lot of people in his line of work were like that. Besides, he came from a big working-class family, and the money he made helped take care of all of them. He took his responsibilities seriously, and he completely understood the fact that getting busted and getting killed are risks that go hand in hand with dealing drugs. Maya's boyfriend, Tito, in particular, was playing at a dangerously high level, and a lot of merchandise passed through his hands. He was always talking about balancing risk and reward. He laid it out for me this way one day: "One point five kilos of cocaine can earn you anywhere from $30,000 to more than $250,000, depending on how you work it and on how many chances you're willing to take."

How is it possible for one quantity of product to translate into such different dollar amounts? "It all depends on how you divide that product up for sale," he explained.

If you sell the product all at once to a single buyer, then you're not going to get much more than $30,000 for it. But if you take that 1.5 kilos and sell it to, say, four different distributors, you might get $20,000 from each, for a total of $80,000. If you divide it even further and dole it out to street dealers, well, you can make quite a bit more. And finally, if you wanted to sell all that coke on the street yourself, it would take you a long time, but that much product has a street value of $250,000 or more.

"It's like a ladder, and each guy at each level has to make a profit, so the price just keeps getting jacked up more and more," Tito went on. "Ultimately, the guy on the street who wants to party has to pay not just for the product but for the work that has been done to get it to him and for the risk that has been taken by a whole lot of people."

That much made sense to me, but since I considered myself a businessman too, I wondered why he wouldn't just eliminate the middlemen. Not all of them, of course, because I knew he'd never stand on a street corner to sell anything, but some of the distributors maybe, so he could make a bigger profit.

The answer was obvious when he said it. It's all about risk. One big sale means one moment of risk: when the transaction takes place and the product is exchanged for money. If you're distributing to several or even hundreds of people, then you risk getting caught each and every time an exchange takes place.

I realized eventually that things aren't so different in my business. The girls who work for me and even my clients are at a much greater risk of getting caught than I am, because I'm nowhere near when money changes hands and the actual sex takes place. I'm safely tucked away in my apartment or hotel room or wherever I happen to be at the time, far from the scene of the crime. When I ran the brothel in New York, I was often there looking after my business while transactions were taking place, and every minute I spent there, I was putting myself at risk of getting arrested. But no more. Of course I have to collect money from my girls eventually, but I don't do it until the pot has grown big enough to merit the risk. Even then, I usually send a go-between to do it for me, and that happens long after all the clients have gone. The police would have to be very patient and dedicated to track any crimes back to me, and frankly, I'm not really worth the trouble. At least, I try not to be.

I admired Tito and the way he thought about things, but he scared me too. He obviously thought of dealing as a long-term business, so he wasn't looking to take too many chances. He had a steady income and made plenty of cash. He knew the price he could pay for getting greedy. But he also never thought about other things he could do to make money that were safer and less stressful for him and for Maya. He was a lifer. There was nothing else for him.

Allen, on the other hand, was more like Andre in that he was interested in other entrepreneurial ventures. And he became even more interested in them as our relationship got more and more serious. He refused to live in the city itself, which he considered far too ghetto, choosing to live in an upscale Maryland suburb instead. I soon found an apartment down the street from him, and Maya and Tito lived across the street from me. Except for the four of us, the neighborhood was entirely white folks. Maya and I reconciled ourselves to living in such an area because at least we had each other, and Maya had kids, so she had her own reasons for wanting to be there. I think Tito and Allen liked it there because it was far enough away from the gang and drug warfare going on all over Baltimore that they felt almost safe and relaxed.

About the time I moved near him, Allen started looking for a way out of the drug business. He had his mind set on buying an upscale "gentlemen's club," one that you could see from the high-way when you were leaving the city. He and Tito and some of their friends used to hang out there. It was our retirement plan. He fig-ured he could quit his business and I could quit mine and together we could run the club, which brought in tons of cash, and lead a legit life from then on. We were gradually building up a stash of cash, which he kept in his apartment, to use as a down payment. We were getting close to having enough when everything turned to shit.

I should have guessed that things were going too well for all of us and that they couldn't last like that forever. I'm a big believer in karma, both in business and in life, and I think that maybe people like me and Allen and Tito and Maya aren't meant to get off that easy. Tito, in particular, had made a lot of enemies, and what goes around, comes around. I don't know how else to explain it.

The tide turned one night without any warning. Allen and I had a fight about the same thing we always fought about: the fact that he was jealous all the time and was holding on to the reins way too tightly. I got so mad that I threw his keys at him (we didn't live together, but we had keys to each other's apartments, which were just a couple minutes' walk apart, so it was almost like we did) and stalked out of his apartment without picking up my purse. When I realized that I didn't have my own keys so I couldn't get back into my apartment, I headed for Maya's place instead. I didn't want to have to face Allen, and I knew Maya would talk me down. She always did.

I was walking through the parking garage of Maya and Tito's apartment complex when I saw them: four black boys in a beat-up old Cadillac speeding toward the exit. Like I said before, this was an exclusive, white neighborhood. You just didn't see people, or cars, like that around there.

I knew right away that something was wrong. As the car passed me, I looked straight at the guys and they looked back at me. I could see them more closely then and by the way they were dressed and the looks on their faces, I knew they were gangsters. I took the elevator up three stories to where Maya had her apartment. It was what they called a "garden-style building," which meant that the hallways leading to the apartments were outside. Each apartment had these sort of frosted glass panels next to the door, which let light into the apartment while still maintaining some privacy from passersby. When I reached Tito and Maya's place, I tried to peek in through their glass, but I could see only the shadowy outlines of things. Then I noticed something on the floor just inside the door. I couldn't see exactly what it was, but it looked big, like it could be a body.

I was on the phone to Maya almost immediately. She was at the local IHOP with her kids and didn't want to bring them home unless she knew it was safe. "You have to call the police," she told me. "You have to."

The cops came right away, along with the some guys from the fire department, who broke down the door. Just as I feared, the shadowy thing I had seen just inside the doorway turned out to be Tito's dead body. The place had been robbed of practically everything of value.

The cops quickly sized up what was going on and called the DEA, who took me to the police station for I don't know how many hours of questions, as if I were the one who had done something wrong. I didn't want to bring trouble to Allen or Maya, so I told them that Tito was a friend of mine who I was just visiting. They could tell I wasn't giving them the full story, but I'd had enough experience with the police by then to know what to say and what not to. When they finally sent me home, alone, they also told me not to leave town. I can't even tell you how fed up I was with government employees by the end of that night.

After that I was on their radar, which meant I had to be really careful about everything. I didn't want them to start looking into my business or Allen's. Still, I was so freaked out by everything that I had to do something to let off steam. So did Maya. A few days after the murder we got a babysitter for her kids, took what money we had, and ran off to Atlantic City in spite of the police's warning.

Maya didn't gamble, but she was such a beauty, she had every high roller throwing money at her for luck. They just wanted her to stand near them while they played, which made her feel a little bit better about everything. I, on the other hand, loved to gamble. I took around $6,000 or $7,000 with me and flipped it into $46,000. It was a great distraction from all the ugly things that were happening for both of us.

When we returned a few days later, Allen was pissed off and the cops had been looking for me. I decided the best thing to do was get a job so I at least looked legit enough to get them off my back. The only problem was that I wasn't qualified to do anything in the real world.

First I worked as a receptionist at a big corporation. It was the most boring thing I've ever done in my life. I cannot overstate how mind-numbingly dull it was. Hour after hour, day after day, I answered phones with fake cheer: "How can I help you?" It was like those were the only words I knew. Then I would transfer the calls to people in the company who were trusted to speak more than that one sentence, although practically everyone else answered the phone using the same stupid line. I don't know how people do shit like that their whole lives. They must want to kill themselves.

When I couldn't take that any longer, I got a job as a waitress. At least that kept me busy and there was a bit of variety to my workdays. When I was a dancer and when I worked other odd jobs over the years, I'd been paid crap wages, but this was the worst. It seemed so unfair that I had to do this when I had been my own boss and had made more money in a couple of weeks than most of the people I was working with would make in a year. There are so many people in this country who work their asses off for shit. In fact, I really believe that the lower your position in life, the more you work and the less you get paid. This country is really fucked up that way.

The restaurant I waitressed at was part of a large chain that marketed themselves as a family establishment offering reasonable prices, which basically translated into demanding customers who left lousy tips. One of their popular promotions was free refills on all nonalcoholic drinks. I was constantly on my feet as it was, but those free refills were what killed me. One day this fat woman asked for so many refills of her and her kids' sodas that I finally got fed up and brought her two big pitchers of the stuff. She got offended and called my manager, who fired me on the spot. Not that I cared. Frankly, I was impressed he did anything at all. He usually sat back and watched football in his office all night, emerging only after we closed to tally up our slips. As for the owner, he was never there, not even once. I pictured him sitting in some grand house somewhere just collecting paychecks for doing nothing. He was probably a guy like my dad.

I managed to live like a relatively legitimate citizen for a while, but overall things were not going well. I was still trying to quietly run my business, but it had really gone to shit. Maya, who had always been my rock and my partner in crime, went a little crazy. She had to get away for a while, so she left town to stay with some relatives. And Allen was too worried about what all the attention from the cops might do to his business to be worried about me. We barely talked to each other anymore.

Then the cops caught Tito's murderers, and things got even worse. It was bearable when those guys thought they'd gotten away with it, but as soon as they were behind bars and I found out the whole story, I couldn't step out my door without looking over my shoulder.

The police caught the idiots because they had kept a bunch of Tito's stuff. They used his cell phone, and one of them had some of Tito's belongings in his car when he got pulled over. Morons. But the guys who did it were just the instruments, not the master-minds. It turned out that it was a gang hit and that Tito's own friend—a guy I'd heard him talk about but had never met—had set him up. For money, nothing more. A big shipment of drugs had recently been busted by the police, so a lot of dealers had run out of product. Tito's friend knew that Tito had a sizable stash of drugs and he wanted it; he had his own friend killed just to get it.

Being the one to discover Tito's body has always made me feel a connection to him for some reason, and thinking back on that time in my life still sends chills down my spine. It's also because sometimes, late at night, when I'm all alone, I even think I can hear him talking to me. No, I'm not crazy, but I do hear voices from time to time. Sometimes Tito's, sometimes my mother's (my birth mother, not the woman who adopted me), and every once in a while, even Natasha's.

Maybe it's my conscience talking to me, or maybe people can speak to you from beyond the grave. I don't know. What I do know is that I often feel like what I hear comes from people who care about me, people who are looking out for me and have my best interests at heart. But not Tito. Some people, after they're gone, if they cared about you, would wish for you to move on with your life and be happy. But Tito, his messages sound more like threats or warnings than anything else.

When I hear him talking to me, it's like he's saying: "Don't you forget about me. Don't you fucking dare." And I haven't. I don't think I ever will.

After his killers were caught, I just couldn't stand it any longer. I was afraid all the time that the guys who had murdered him were coming back for me. I knew they had seen me, I just knew it. And even though the guys who did it were convicted and got the death penalty, Tito's friend, the one who planned it all, never was caught. Besides, they were gang members, and gang members stick together, which means there's always someone who can come after you. I couldn't sleep. I could barely eat. Maya was gone, and Allen and I were practically strangers. I had no reason to stay. In fact, I had every reason to go.

I didn't know what I was going to do or where to go; I just knew I needed to get away. Maya and I had had such a good time in Atlantic City and I loved gambling so much that that was the first place I thought of. There's something calming about betting, because I can focus completely on the game and everything else leaves my head. That was exactly what I needed right then. Once I had decided to go, I just took off without looking back. I didn't care about Allen or about the cops, who still wanted me to stay in town. I didn't care about my things or about the money Allen and I had put away. I didn't care about much of anything except getting somewhere where I didn't have to be scared all the time. I took all the money I could easily get my hands on, including my winnings from my last trip, and I just played.

My game is blackjack, and I went from casino to casino playing night after night for five weeks. The whole period is mostly a blur. When I gamble, I gamble hard, and at that point in my life I gambled harder than ever before. Pretty soon I had lost nearly everything I had.

I remember, after almost all my money was gone, waking up in my car because I couldn't afford a room. Once again, I knew it was time to move on. I was tired of being there. Besides, Atlantic City is no fun when you're broke. I knew I wasn't ready to settle down again just yet, and, for me, the only way to avoid that was to keep moving. So that's what I did.

CHAPTER 7

My Canadian Escape

I arrived in Montreal with a change of clothes stuffed into a back-pack and my fur coat over my arm. That's all I thought I needed. Montreal was supposed to be a short vacation—a chance to figure out what to do next and an escape from the last place I'd escaped to—but somehow I ended up staying in Canada for four years.

I got to Montreal by borrowing a car from Jack, a big-time player from NYC. He was a good friend of Andre's, but I had actually met him even before Andre and I started going out. He used to come into the strip clubs where I danced when I was living with Jackson. He would often give me weed, which made me think he was just a petty weed dealer. I later found out that he was one of the biggest hustlers around.

When it was time to leave Atlantic City, I had almost no money and nowhere to go. Jack helped me through a rough spot, but not without strings attached. He had wanted me from the first time he saw me years ago. Even though he was powerful and ready to come to my aid, I also thought he was one of the most disgusting-looking guys I'd ever seen in my life. Once I didn't need him any-more, I couldn't get away from him fast enough.

I got him to loan me his car by telling him I was going to visit my family for the weekend. I ended up in Montreal because I knew he couldn't follow me there. He was one of the main sus-pects in a high-profile murder at the time and wasn't allowed to leave the country. Once I was there, I had someone drive the car back over the border and leave it in a parking garage. Then I called Jack and left him a message telling him where he could find his car and that I wouldn't be coming back after all.

Things started off okay in Montreal. I was on my own, so life was pretty relaxed—no one working for me, no one living with me, no real attachments of any kind. I danced now and then at a local club to make some money, but most of the time I just hung out and did whatever I felt like. I started casually dating a stripper, which was new to me since I had never really just dated before. I'd always had boyfriends, one powerful guy after another, who had taken care of me, taught me what I needed to know about life, about business, and about getting by. Not that any of them would ever have taught me directly how to be independent. In fact, they were all quick to tell me that I couldn't do anything without them, but I had learned just by being around them. By the time I got to Canada, I didn't feel like belonging to anyone anymore, and I now knew that I didn't need to.

Then I met Charles. He caught my attention at a local bar where I used to gamble on the Loto-Québec machines. The bar was right next to 281, the hottest male strip club in Canada. Girls used to line up for blocks on a Friday night just to get in. This was Saint Catherine Street, where you could find, and buy, just about any type of sin, and there was at least one church and one bar on every block.

Charles was adorable, very cocky and confident. He had this way of keeping his distance from people while, at the same time, making himself known to everyone. We'd run into each other a number of times along Saint Catherine but had not really spoken much. I'd been keeping my eye on him though.

One night, the stripper and I had a date that ended early, so I asked him to drop me off at the bar afterward. He had just left when Charles walked up to me.

"I see you only date pretty boys," he said, as if it were an accusa-tion. I took it as a compliment and shrugged.

"You're pretty enough," I said. "Why haven't you asked me out yet?"

He did, of course, and I knew right then and there that I would never see the stripper again. The stripper was fun and, more important, head-turningly gorgeous, but Charles, well, I just thought he had so much potential.

Pretty soon I had moved out of the hotel where I was staying and into Charles's small studio apartment. It was located right out-side the city in a not-so-great part of town. Charles was on proba-tion, so the first thing he did was school me on what to say if, for example, the phone rang after a certain hour of the day and he wasn't home. (I was always supposed to say he was sleeping or in the shower unless it was someone I knew.) The studio was run-down, with a tiny kitchen and an even tinier bathroom. Charles had only the bare essentials to get by and nothing more.

Charles was a drug dealer, but compared to the guys I had dated before, he was strictly small-time. Most nights he'd stand on a corner on Saint Catherine Street selling small pieces of rock wrapped in tinfoil for twenty dollars each. If the cops came, he'd put the foil in his mouth, and if they really bothered him, he'd swallow it. The penalties for selling drugs were very high in Canada, especially for a repeat offender, and Charles was deter-mined not to go back to jail.

Occasionally Charles's pager would go off and he'd hop into a cab to make a delivery, often for just forty to sixty dollars. Most of his clients were worn-out prostitutes and junkies. I watched him for a while before deciding that I was going to help him. I had to. His way of doing business was like climbing a mountain with no equipment . . . it was going to take forever for him to get any-where. If he was going to make any real money, then things needed to change right away.

I made pretty good money dancing, and since I was living at his place and didn't have a business of my own anymore, my expenses were practically nothing. So I decided to help Charles out the same way my Andre had helped me, by putting up the money and showing him how to really do business the right way.

I gave Charles the money he needed to buy a larger quantity of product, which, I explained to him, meant he could get more for his money. Now he could supply the boys who worked the corners on Saint Catherine with him or, better yet, get those boys to work for him exclusively.

"This is how things should work," I told him. "Go to those boys and tell them that you'll supply them with their product from now on for the same price that they were paying before, only for every five pieces of rock they sell, they'll get one for free. This will be their incentive, both to keep buying from you and to sell more stuff, and the more they sell, the happier everyone will be. And no more standing out on the street waiting for people to come to you. It's too dangerous. You can keep the customers you already have, but from now on, they have to call and wait for you. And you have a hundred-dollar minimum for deliveries. If they don't like it, fuck 'em. You don't need to be running around town for small-time customers anymore."

Pretty soon Charles was making a lot more money with a lot less risk. He got to the point where he had five employees working for him, and they were the ones standing out on the street selling every night. All Charles had to do was make sure they were fully stocked with product so that the money would always flow. He hardly had to work at all. Most of the time he stayed home or went out and played. Business was safer, easier, *and* he made more money. Why would you do it any other way?

Charles was a good student. He listened carefully and did everything I said. He didn't have the attitude that Andre or Allen had, so he didn't have a problem taking advice from me as long as

I didn't give it to him in front of anyone else. But not having an attitude can be a liability in this line of work, so I had to teach him about Respect, with a capital *R,* too. I started by giving him his first gangster nickname. I began calling him Capone, after my childhood hero.

Everyone we knew and everyone around us was some type of hustler—pimps, hookers, dealers, gamblers, junkies, gangsters . . . you name it, they were around. That was the world we lived in, and the problem with that is, as soon as you have something of your own, someone is going to be there to try to take it from you. Charles was suddenly in a place where he had something to lose.

As for me, I had made my stand early on, when I had first arrived in Montreal, so that people knew right off the bat not to mess with me. I had been at my favorite bar sitting by myself holding a beer in one hand and playing the poker machine with the other when a chubby blonde who had been sitting with a bunch of girls came up to me.

"You need to get a pimp in your life," she said, no doubt at the prompting of her own pimp, who was looking to recruit some more "talent."

I kept my eyes on my game as I responded, "Why don't you go suck somebody's dick and get out of my face."

I obviously offended her with that comment, and she started screaming at me: "Who do you think you are? You can't talk to me like that!"

So I picked up one of the nearby bar stools and went after her, chasing her through the bar like a madwoman. In a situation like this one, it didn't make that much difference if I beat her or she beat me. It's the way you fight that matters. There are certain unwritten rules. Don't pull hair. Weapons are fine. Just keep going until someone stops you, someone can't get up, or you hear the sound of sirens. And if you do hear sirens, just walk away as if nothing ever happened, no matter what you look like, even if your ribs are broken and there's blood streaming down your face. You can never let them see you hurting. And if you get knocked on your ass, you have to get back up again and keep punching. That's the way to let people know that you can't be taken down.

My fight with the blonde was split up pretty quickly, but from that point on, everyone knew I wasn't the type to take any shit. It was a small world that we lived in and word traveled fast.

I told Charles that he was going to have to make an impression too, one that said loud and clear that he wasn't to be messed with. "Since you're a guy and a real drug dealer now, you're going to have to send an even stronger message," I told him.

His chance came when I got into a fight with the girlfriend of one of the kids who worked for him. The guy was barely eighteen, but he thought he was a real pimp. His girlfriend was twenty-four and a stripper at one of the local clubs. He always took all her money and spent it on gambling or on trying to get laid. He threw it away like it grew on trees. I used to play pool with him because he was an easy mark and I always knew I could quickly take some of his money for myself.

One night, after I had gone double or nothing with him several times—winning every game, of course—I asked his girlfriend why the fuck she would give her money away to a loser like him.

"My man is the best man in the world," she said. "He treats me like a queen. Whatever I want, he gets it for me. It doesn't get any better than him."

I had to laugh at that. This girl didn't have a car, she wore the same outfit every week and lived in a tiny apartment where the heat barely worked. The bitch needed to be checked, so I told her, loudly, "You stupid cunt, your man is a whore. I see him chasing a different girl every night while you're out working to make the money that *he* takes from you and then quickly loses half of to me because he sucks at pool. And if he's such a big pimp, why is he working for my man?"

I knew that would start a fight between us, and it did. The girl could really throw a punch, and I went home that night with knots all over my head. I told Charles that he had better do something about this before the girl's boyfriend got it in his head that he could do whatever he wanted. It was all bullshit really, but it was an opportunity for Charles to publicly let people know that he was not to be messed with, nor was anyone close to him.

The next night Charles tracked down the girl and her boyfriend at the bar and pistol-whipped them both in front of everyone. Soon after, I ran into the girlfriend again and got right in her face. To my surprise she just walked away. Charles had apparently made his point. Neither she nor her boyfriend ever talked shit around either of us again.

Our lifestyle improved after that, but our relationship just got worse and worse. Quite frankly, in making Charles over in the image of my past loves—in my own image, really, since I had become what they had taught me to be—I'd made him into a monster.

Things really got bad when I started teaching him how to run girls. There is a difference between running girls and being a pimp, but Charles couldn't see that. And if he was going to act like a pimp around his girls, then guess what he was going to act like around his girlfriend. He conveniently forgot the fact that I had taught him practically everything he knew. Some people have no class that way.

I finally left Charles for good when I found out that he had been dipping into the $200,000 we had saved as our "retirement fund." He blew the money on trips to the casino and $1,500 games of pool, which was a disastrous way for him to try to make money since I beat him at pool every time we played and I was no pool shark (though I wasn't bad either). When I heard what he'd been doing, I demanded he open the safe where we kept the money. I found only $30,000 inside.

I left Charles the money, telling him to use it to get a decent education since he wasn't going to make it on his own any other way. Instead I took all the jewelry he'd given me and went straight to the pawnshop. I didn't get much money for it, not compared to the amount I left Charles with, but it was enough to start over.

Unfortunately, Charles wasn't so easy to leave. He followed me places and threatened me and whoever I was with. One time he even tried to strangle me outside of a gambling bar. I got away from him and ran to Audrey's place. Audrey was the only friend I'd made in Montreal, and we'd spent a lot of time together even though Charles hated her.

Audrey was a total drug addict, but I thought she was cool anyway. She was a renegade ho who worked entirely on her own. She used to have a pimp, but he had turned into a junkie and couldn't look out for her anymore. It was a good thing that he had loved her enough to let her go, because most pimps would have dragged her down with them. She was the perfect person to come to my rescue, because not only was she independent but she was out of control, so much so that even Charles was a bit scared of her.

Still, the harassment continued until one day I picked up a copy of *Allô Police,* which is a local magazine with stories about the most notorious crimes and criminals in Quebec. It's not the type of thing that I usually like to read, but I picked it up this time because Charles's picture was on the cover. He'd gotten busted in our old apartment, and they were charging him with possession of lots and lots of weed and cocaine.

I thought it was kind of funny, until the cops came searching for me. They were having problems making their charges stick and they wanted me to testify. Luckily, Charles had a good lawyer (a crooked Jewish guy who I had used once before and who had so many criminal clients, he could get you practically any illegal goods or services that you could possibly want), and I wouldn't have dreamed of testifying against him. It's not that I was afraid of what Charles would have done if I did, it was more that it was against my code. Instead, I made up a story that completely muddled their case, and then I ran so they could never call me into court. I bought a ticket to Ontario, where I knew a couple of girls who danced in clubs and could get me a job doing the same to tide myself over for a while.

I spent an entire year in hiding in a place called Thunder Bay. I don't know if you've ever been to Thunder Bay, but if you haven't, don't go. It's one of the most boring places I've ever been in my life. Near the top of Lake Superior, it has maybe 100,000 people living there, nearly all of them white, spread across this semi-suburban, semi-wilderness area where there is almost nothing to do. In fact, the area boasts a big park and a marina as its main tourist attractions, but since it snows there like half the year and it's cold even when it's not snowing, who'd want to hang out outside in places like that? I played bingo every evening before work just for thrills. In fact, practically everyone there plays bingo. It's one of the region's highlights. I made a few friends, who got me into ecstasy, which I loved, but that's basically all I did for fun for an entire year—play bingo and take ecstasy. When I finally got the news that they'd dropped the charges and Charles was off the hook, I couldn't wait to get back to civilization.

I took the bus back to Montreal since I hardly had any money left by then. Thanks to the facts that it was tough to make money in the backwoods of Ontario and that there was hardly anything to do but gamble, I hadn't been able to save much. Still, I didn't care. In fact, I was so happy to be back that I wasn't worried about anything. One of the first things I did was contact Charles. I didn't know how he was going to feel about hearing from me, so I left him a message saying, "I lost an entire year of my life to keep you safe, and if you still want to kill me, just do it, because I am not running away anymore." Then I told him where I'd be that night and to "come and get me" if he really wanted to.

Charles showed up that night all right. And he gave me the biggest hug of my life. Turned out he was grateful for what I'd done to keep him out of jail. "I love you no matter what," he said. He hardly had any money either, thanks to all his legal expenses, but he'd just started hustling again and he gave me a couple hundred bucks toward getting my life back together. I was so relieved to be back and not to have to worry about him trying to hurt me anymore that I started to cry. I was on my own again and it felt good.

Soon after I came back to Montreal, I met Philippe. He was the kind of guy who could make a guy like Charles just fade into the background. Philippe was a beautiful little dancer who worked at several strip clubs for men around the city. He was totally gorgeous, and he knocked me off my feet the first time I saw him. I knew right away that I wanted to go home with him, but what I didn't know was that I'd end up falling for him.

The night we met I was at girls' night at one of the gay clubs where Philippe worked. The gay clubs would open their doors to women one or two nights a week because they always had the hottest-looking guys working there, and ladies would line up around the block to get in. I saw Philippe dancing for some girl and thought he was adorable. I wanted him to dance for me too, so I gave twenty dollars to another dancer and asked him to get Philippe for me. I waited for him, but to my surprise, Philippe never came over. I watched as he danced for two more girls and then said, "Fuck him," and decided to leave with my friends. As I was heading toward the door, Philippe finally came over and asked me what I was doing later. "Coming to get you," I said, trying not to blush. My friends were all giggling behind me.

I really just wanted a little affection. At 3:00 A.M., when Philippe was due to get off work, I drove up to the club, and there he was standing outside. He smiled at me with these big dimples as he got into the car.

We ended up taking some ecstasy together late and then couldn't keep our hands off each other. We were both instantly in love and checked into one of those cheesy motels with heart-shaped water beds and Jacuzzis in every room. To this day I remember that as one of the most passionate nights of my life. Philippe and I spent every night together for the next six months after that.

During the course of that first night, I was flirting with Philippe and told him that I ran an escort agency. It sounded better than being a part-time dancer and a dealer's ex-girlfriend, and I wanted to impress him. It worked. I definitely had his attention after that, but the truth was I hadn't run girls since I was in Baltimore. After what happened there, I hadn't been in too much of a hurry to get back into business for myself and deal with that kind of responsibility. At the time, the fact that I was kind of lying didn't matter to me because my plan was to have a one-night stand—my first ever, since I'd been a serial monogamist up until then—and never see the guy again.

The thing that bothers me the most about love is how hard it is to control. The next morning I realized how much I actually liked Philippe. I didn't want him to think I was a liar, so I decided the only thing I could do was make my lie true by starting up a new business. I figured I could use some more money anyway. Ignoring the fact that I had no clients and no employees, I threw up a quarter-page ad in one of the local skin magazines advertising my new agency. Twenty-four hours later I was in business.

The ad for what I was calling my University Escorts service not only attracted customers, it attracted girls looking for work, just like when I opened my New York brothel. I started out by offering better-than-average rates so that I could lure some of the best girls away from other employers. It totally worked. After the first week I had ten girls ready to work for me.

Starting up may have been easy, but staying in business was hard. At the time the going rate in Montreal was $140 Canadian for an hour-long appointment. Of that, $70 to $80 typically went to the girl (or her pimp, as was often the case there), and $20 went to the driver who brought her to her appointment, leaving only $50 or less for the agency. And with the better rates I was offering girls, I often got even less than that. It was chump change.

The problem was $140 was all most of the locals could afford to pay. On top of that, competition was fierce. In a pretty small city, there were over three hundred agencies to choose from, many of which were run by biker gangs, who had the local French-speaking market pretty much sewn up. So if you tried to charge more, guys would just go somewhere else. A lot of agencies even offered discounts to survive, advertising girls at as low as $120 an hour. At those rates, with my gambling habit (sometimes I lost as much as $5,000 a week), I'd have had to work myself silly to make a decent living.

Everyone else around me just accepted these standards, but I decided I needed to figure out something better. Experience had shown me that Americans were willing to pay a lot more, so I figured the only real money would be in marketing to tourists. I started taking out ads in American newspapers and tourist magazines.

Unfortunately, I soon discovered that there weren't enough tourists to sustain the business, and I knew that if I didn't keep my girls working, they'd leave me just as they'd left their last agencies in search of something better. So in order to keep things going, I had to appeal to both the wealthier tourists and the cheap locals at the same time. That's when I came up with the idea of having different categories of girls at different prices.

I called my service University Escorts because I planned to market my girls as if they were all young coeds just discovering their sexuality, the kind who went to school during the day and partied hard at night. I kept that $140 price point that everyone else around me was charging, labeling those girls "Sexy Classmates." That was the low-end category. In the middle I had "The Honor Roll," a smaller group of higher-class girls who were more experienced and gave better service for a rate of $200 an hour. Then we had our "Teachers' Pets," who went for $250 to $300; we usually rolled out this category when there was a big event or convention in town that attracted lots of tourists. And every month I'd feature a different "Student of the Month," a luxurious treat for $500.

The secret was that there really was no difference among the categories. I used the same girls to fill all levels, depending on who was available when a call came in. Still, it worked. The marketing gimmick attracted customers of all types. There was something for everyone. Most important, it made those willing to pay more feel like they were getting something extra special for their money, which made them more inclined to use my service instead of another one. I still had to hustle, but during a good week I made $5,000 for myself. That was much better than the $1,000 per week I had been making when I first started out dancing in Montreal.

I wasn't very fair to my girls back then. I figured that their job was pretty much the same regardless of what the client was paying, so when I got a higher-paying client, I pocketed the extra myself. After all, if the girls were willing to take $80 or less per customer before, then they would still take it now. Don't forget, I started out paying them more than the other agencies did. But since the girls were the ones who collected the money, they knew what was happening, and I began to get complaints from some of them. Sometimes, to make a girl happy, I would pay her a small bonus over what she was used to getting when she was working as a "Teachers' Pet" or "Student of the Month," but it was really just a token amount.

If I had to do it all over again, I would pay the girls more. The truth is they deserved it. I used only local girls then, and Montreal girls are very hardworking. Because they have a more European sensibility, they also tend to be more uninhibited and very sexy. There are so many adorable little French girls there, it's no wonder that there's so much prostitution. I had one very finicky client who liked only girls who weighed under one hundred pounds. He would even bring a scale with him to the hotel and make the girl stand on it before he paid her. I can think of maybe one or two American girls I've worked with over the years who would be able to satisfy his fetish, but there, I could almost always find someone he'd be happy with every time he called. I bring in girls from Montreal to work for me to this day because they tend to be so good at their jobs.

The saddest part of it all was that I could get away with paying girls less in Montreal no matter how good they were because the trade there was mostly run by pimps, who barely paid them anything. I came to realize that if I had paid them better, they probably would have given better service and that could have meant more repeat business, which would have made my job a lot easier because I wouldn't have to be reaching out to new tourists all the time. But even more than that, as I've said, I believe in karma, and I think the way I treated the girls back then lost me some points in that area. Now I give my girls a standard percentage of the price of each appointment no matter what it is, so that if I make more, they do too. I wasn't doing business the right way in Montreal, but at least I learned from my mistakes, and now I believe in always sharing the wealth.

That wasn't the only thing I learned during that time. It was while I was in Montreal that I took the first step toward the future of my business: I learned how to use a computer. This was the mid- to late-1990s, when the Internet was starting to really take hold. Some agencies were beginning to advertise on the Web, so, to get a leg up in such a competitive market, I decided I should too. I like to learn new things, so I taught myself how to use a computer and started my very first Web site for my University Escorts.

The sex industry has obviously taken full advantage of the Internet revolution practically since the day it started. In fact, it's probably more technologically advanced than a lot of industries, so if I wanted my business to stay competitive, I had to keep up. Besides that, I don't know if I would still be in the business today if I hadn't been able to go completely high-tech. I think back to my days in New York and I can't believe I ever survived those times. My very first experience there with Julio and Natasha in Times Square or those first brothels that Suzie and I opened on West Twenty-first Street . . . we were like sitting ducks then, easily picked up by any policeman who cared to make the effort. At that time, the police just didn't care enough to go out of their way to shut businesses like mine down for good. Today things are different. I'd never put myself out there like that. Fortunately, technology has made it so I don't have to ever again.

It used to be that the trade in any major city was generally contained in one or several neighborhoods. That meant that people like me were tied to a physical location. When I moved to Montreal, the city still had its unofficially designated neighborhood where you knew you could find a girl on a street corner or in a bar, but thanks to my Web site, I didn't need to spend any time in those places unless I wanted to.

In Baltimore, I hadn't needed a physical space, like a brothel, to work out of either, but I also wasn't doing anything illegal, not to mention the fact that I wasn't making all that much money compared to what I make now. Montreal was midway in my evolution into a virtual business. I no longer needed to rent a space for my girls to work out of because customers could find us through my Web site and then I could send the girls out to meet them wherever they were. But still, because technology wasn't so advanced in those days, I had to be there. I had to be in the city to find girls to work for me. I had to meet with them to make sure they looked the part. I had a clunky computer, a landline, and a fax machine that I used to do business, all of which meant I needed a space to plug in and work somewhere in or near the city itself.

Back then I also split my efforts between print and online ads, but today I don't even bother with anything that I can't do on my own with my laptop. I run my business using two cell phones, one with an 800 number, a Web site on an offshore server that shows pictures of the girls who are available each week, and an e-mail address that customers can use to request appointments twenty-four hours a day (and I probably don't even need that much to be successful). If a new girl wants to work for me, she can e-mail me pictures and I can check reviews of her past work online. No one ever needs to know what I look like or even where I am in order to do business with me. I have even run my agency in New Jersey from the beach in Florida or Mexico for weeks at a time without anyone knowing the difference.

All this means that today I can work from just about anywhere. In fact, moving around a lot is part of how I keep myself safe. It used to be that, if I moved to a new town, I also had to shut down my business and start over in the new location. Not anymore. When I move, my business travels with me. I could be living and working right next door to you and you wouldn't even know it. I used to know of this agency that ran out of a big office building in midtown Manhattan. It was one of those places with lots of office suites in the heart of the city's business district. There were probably hundreds of companies in the same building, and not a single one had a clue what was going on right next to them until one day the cops showed up and busted the place. And the cops probably only found the place because they stayed there for too long. Not me. I work from wherever I'm living at the time—whether it's a hotel room, an apartment, a boyfriend's house, or wherever—and live off the grid as much as possible. That means that I pay for practically everything in cash instead of using credit cards, I get friends to lease apartments or cars for me in their own names (I usually have to pay them for the favor, but it's worth it), and I even have a fake ID with a made-up name that I use when checking into hotels and things like that. All of it, the mobility and the anonymity, keeps me safer than ever before.

I stuck with University Escorts for two and a half years before closing it down. That was a good run for me back then, especially considering the conditions I was working under. Competition was always fierce in Montreal, and the agency I was running was more straight sex, not the GFE-style (girlfriend experience) service I run today, so I was never able to build up much of a regular clientele. Still, it wasn't business considerations that caused me to hang it up, it was my boyfriend Philippe.

Although he was impressed with the idea of me being a madam when we first met, he didn't actually like the reality of what I did. Trying to make a business like mine work can be all-consuming. Once the business started to take off, I'd be on the phone or the computer for hours at a time and until all hours of the night. Philippe had nothing against the nature of my business, and he didn't mind that I worked hard—well, maybe he felt a bit neglected sometimes—but mostly, he was just worried about me. In case you haven't figured it out already, I have a pretty obsessive personality, and when I get an idea in my head—like when I wanted to learn how to build my own Web site so I didn't have to pay someone else to do it, or when I came up with a new marketing strategy that I was dying to try—I couldn't stop myself from working until I saw results. I'm still that way, as are, I think, most good business owners.

I had also developed a big speed addiction by then. The speed I got in Canada was nothing like what you get in the United States. It was a dream drug. I would take one pill, then another half every three to four hours and feel like I had woken up from a perfect night's sleep even though I had never gone to bed. It was almost euphoric. Unfortunately, I did this for years, which eventually fucked up my system. I wouldn't be able to sleep for five days straight until, all of a sudden, I'd crash. Then Philippe wouldn't be able to wake me up for two days, no matter what he did. And even worse from Philippe's perspective was the fact that, when I was on a binge, I'd just keep on working all night long. He wasn't as into drugs as I was then. In fact, our first night together, when we took ecstasy, it was the first time he'd ever done it.

Finally, Philippe asked me to quit the business. We'd been together so long—more than two years, which was a long time for me, anyway—that I took him seriously and made a deal. "I'll quit my job if you quit yours," I said. He was still dancing, and I didn't love the idea of other men and women fantasizing about him on a regular basis. I told you he was gorgeous, and I didn't have to actually see people hit on him to know that they were, all the time.

Philippe agreed, and we became quite the little domestic couple after that. We had enough money to get by on for a while, so we just played house together. Pretty soon I found out that I was pregnant, and Philippe was thrilled. His excitement was short-lived, however, because I had a miscarriage early in the pregnancy.

Things degenerated between us after that for a lot of reasons. In the end I think we were just too different. I decided I really needed to build my business back up again to make some money. Thanks to a number of unpaid traffic tickets for moving violations, I ended up getting arrested and owing the government around $4,000. I also had to fork over a bunch in bail money to get myself out of jail. I was dead broke, and still Philippe didn't want me to go back to work.

We argued about it all the time, and I finally had to admit to myself that the reasons why I was so set on getting back to work had to do with more than just money. I actually *wanted* to get back into business. I was only in my mid-twenties, so I couldn't imagine being retired for the rest of my life. Besides, I felt lost and a little bit worthless without work to do. That made me realize that I had some demon thoughts in my head I needed to confront. I had always had this feeling that, if Philippe really knew me, he would hate me. If he truly understood that I was part of this world because I wanted to be and not just because I didn't have many other choices, I knew he would think a lot less of me. Whenever I thought like this, I'd decide that our love was a lie. I loved him, but he couldn't possibly love me, not the real me. We ended up breaking up because there just wasn't any way that it could possibly work.

I still consider Philippe to be my one true love and soul mate. I loved Andre and Allen, but with Philippe things were different. He was truly a sweet soul and he cared about what was best for *me* first, not for himself, not for business, not for anything else. I trusted him more than I've ever trusted anyone. I sometimes wonder what my life would be like now if things had turned out differently between us, but it was probably never meant to be. I just don't think a stable relationship is in the cards for someone like me. I've never believed that I was the type to get married or have kids. But still, Philippe was special.

Philippe took our breakup really hard. He stalked me for a while and would show up at my apartment at random hours of the day and night. Once I even found him passed out on my doorstep when I woke up in the morning. His friend Rick, who worked as a bartender at one of the strip clubs where Philippe used to dance, had always been into me, so I decided that the best way to put permanent distance between Philippe and me was to hook up with his friend. Rick and I started dating, and Philippe was furious, but he also finally got it through his head that things between us were over for good.

Staying in Montreal after things with Philippe died out was probably a mistake, but I had lost my ID, so I didn't have any way to cross the border back into the United States. I'm sure I could have found a way, but I didn't. The world seemed to be telling me it was time to move on, and I just wasn't listening.

CHAPTER 8

My Canadian Escape, Part 2

Life in Canada after Philippe consisted mostly of working, gambling, and dating. Those were the three basics in my life. I was making decent money, still about $5,000 a week, which could go a long way in Canada, except that I lost about that much each week in my favorite local casino. It didn't help that I started dating the city's best card counter, who loved going to the casino almost as much as I did. He was a mathematician and a teacher, a real nerd and not like the guys I usually dated, but I liked him and we had some fun together.

I also made some friends and contacts that I still have to this day. As I've said, I bring in a lot of girls from Montreal to work for my current agency because they are experienced and really good at their jobs. My friend Nicky, for example, who worked for me then and still does sometimes, is barely five feet tall, looks about fifteen even though she's much older than that, and has natural DD breasts. You'd think she'd be hunching over all the time from carrying so much weight up top, but she's a firecracker. Back then she had pink hair and a pierced tongue and went everywhere with a tiny *Powerpuff Girls* backpack on her back. Guys loved her then, and they love her now. She's white, but she has the sultry voice of a big black woman and has always had dreams of becoming a singer. She could probably make it too, if she just got off the fucking mescaline.

I also got to know some other agency owners in the area. After September 11, 2001, tourism really slowed down in Montreal. Only the strong survived that downturn, and with my gambling habit, I just couldn't hold out. So I shut down my agency. I started working for one of the top five agencies in the city (I was only in the top twenty when I closed shop), which had enough local clients to sustain itself until things picked up again. I had become amazing at working the phones and booking appointments, so when I shut down my own business, Doug, the owner of that agency, offered me a job.

I got a commission on each booking I made. I would usually just work from home, but on busy nights I'd ride along with the drivers who brought girls to and from their appointments to make sure everything went smoothly. It was a lot less pressure than having my own business, so I kind of liked it for a while. It was like taking a semi-vacation.

A booking girl's salary, however, wasn't what I'd been used to. Pretty soon I couldn't pay rent on my luxury apartment. Doug had a girlfriend named Sandy, who had been trying to befriend me ever since I started working for him. I didn't really trust her, but when she offered to let me stay with her for a while, I figured it was a good temporary solution. I think the real reason she wanted me to move in was because she wanted a full-time babysitter for her kids. In any case, that's exactly what I became.

Sandy had four kids, two by her previous husband, who lived with her, and two by the husband before that, who she saw every other weekend and on holidays. She was a real bitch. Before I got there, the kids ate cereal for breakfast, lunch, and dinner. Once in a while, on special occasions, she'd make them mac and cheese out of a box, which was the only thing she knew how to cook. When she wanted them to do something for her, she'd bribe them with candy, which almost always worked since they were always hungry. And that was when she was around. She was always running off with different guys to go shopping, leaving the kids home to fend for themselves.

It's not like she ever asked me to babysit, but I couldn't stand to see her treat her kids like that, so I started taking care of them. Besides, I was there and she wasn't. I cooked dinner for them and packed them lunches for school. The two who lived with us full-time were real problem kids. When they were upset, I'd ask them to draw pictures of something that would make them happy. One of the boys once drew his ideal living situation. It was a house with him, his brother, and his dad together on one side of the house and his mother all by herself way on the other side. He hated his mother. As hard as I tried not to, I couldn't help myself, and I fell in love with those kids.

Meanwhile, Sandy's kids weren't the only ones she was being a bitch to. She had taken over a lot of the daily work of running the agency (with my help, of course), so Doug hardly knew what was going on anymore. Every chance she got she robbed him blind. She'd make excuses, like they'd had a lean week, and then pocket the cash for herself. She was robbing me too, and the problem was, I knew it. She gave me only about one-tenth of what she owed me in booking commissions, most of which I would spend on decent food for her kids.

I didn't respect Sandy, but I did learn something from her: always keep an eye on your business. During my most successful periods, I'm often tempted to hire someone to do some of the grunt work for me, particularly answering the phones. But when I remember Sandy, I know it's better not to trust anyone with too much information about my business. Doug was a good enough guy. I didn't know him that well, but he did help me out when I needed work and I liked him. But he should have known better. Particularly when Colonel Ed showed up. Ed was an ex-military guy who introduced himself as an expert in targeted Internet mailing lists. He did this kind of work for a whole range of industries actually, not just escort agencies, so most of the time Colonel Ed ran a legitimate business. He was the one who found us, called us up, and asked if we were interested in expanding.

Colonel Ed claimed to have a way of reaching out to a bigger client base who would be particularly interested in the services we offered. He had somehow—I'm not sure exactly how—gathered an extensive list of e-mail addresses for likely customers we could contact directly. When Sandy heard about this, you could just see the dollar signs in her eyes. She did her best to keep Colonel Ed away from Doug, and she did a pretty good job. It didn't seem to occur to her, however, to keep Colonel Ed away from me.

Since I was doing most of the work booking appointments, Colonel Ed would often talk to me about business. It wasn't long before he realized that it made much more sense to leave Sandy out of things whenever possible. She was unstable and he knew it. He wasn't looking to get busted, so he preferred to deal with me. I came across as much more grounded by comparison.

Basically what Ed proposed was that we send out e-mail announcements to his mailing list and then he would take a fee for every appointment we booked for guys on his list. It turned out that he actually did have something worthwhile to sell, and the business always got a boost whenever we sent out an e-mail. I learned from talking to Colonel Ed that he also had contact lists for other places, in the United States. That's what made me realize that it was finally time, past time really, to make a change.

One day a request came in from a new client who wanted a girl for companionship only, no sex. He was a businessman passing through town who just didn't feel like being alone. When I saw that he'd asked specifically for an Asian girl, I jumped at the chance to take the call myself. He was offering good money for easy work, and I wanted it.

The guy's name was Paul, and he had some serious mental issues, one of which was a real fear of women. He paid $2,000 to have dinner with me and then go out clubbing. He even showed up with a pair of diamond earrings as a gift, as if it was a real date. I was happy to take them, even though I thought he was pretty pathetic to do something like that. I got him high as hell at the nightclub and then left his ass early that night.

After that, Paul was hooked on me. I guess he liked women who treated him badly. Normally I would have brushed him off, but in this case, I saw an opportunity. He was the perfect guy to help me get back into the United States.

I'd been reluctant to try to cross the border alone, because after September 11 security was tighter than ever and I still didn't have an ID. Besides that, I was still out on bail for those moving violations. I'd never shown up to court and never paid my fine. If anyone looked up my record, they were sure to catch me and send me back to jail.

I hadn't wanted to take any form of public transportation back to the United States because they tended to inspect people's IDs more closely at airports and train stations. I figured I might be able to get away with just flashing a fake ID at the border guards if I was in a private car. Paul had a BMW, and he offered to drive me to Boston, which was where I wanted to end up. I decided it was worth the risk. Before I left, however, I called child services and told them that all Sandy's kids would be better off with their dads. I did it for the kids' safety. I was really sad to leave them behind. I also contacted Doug and told him what Sandy had been doing behind his back. I made that call because the bitch deserved it.

My plan for getting over the border worked like a charm. Paul was a real businessman and he had a nice car, so the border guard trusted us and let us through. Once I got to Boston, however, I ditched Paul as quickly as I could. I already had other plans, and he wasn't part of them.

My Boston plans revolved around a guy named Master Romeo. That was his screen name anyway. He was (and still is) a key player on the most well-known escort review Web sites out there. These review sites are independent, so people tend to trust the general consensus of opinion that emerges about a girl or an agency, the same way they do customer reviews of books on Amazon or restaurant reviews in Zagat. Beyond that, however, certain reviewers have become famous on the sites. They're unpaid, just like any other reviewer, but because of the depth of their experience and the way they turn a phrase, their reviews have attracted followings among like-minded men. Master Romeo and a select group of other reviewers have serious cachet with a whole lot of clients and potential clients of services like mine throughout the country and in Canada. They've developed reputations as "experts," and their screen names are known throughout the community of "hobbyists," as they often call themselves. Their reviews of the girls they've "dated" can even make or break careers. In fact, if I have a new girl who's not booking many appointments, I'll sometimes offer her to one of these guys for free in the very real hope that a good review, which acts almost like a celebrity endorsement, might kick-start her career.

Master Romeo and I had become friends in Montreal, and I made him an ally when I decided it was time to leave town. I knew that he and several other all-star reviewers were also members of an exclusive club of very wealthy Boston men. The club sponsored regular parties, and for each one they hired lots and lots of working girls to attend. They often used a big agency called Montreal Girlfriends to provide them with the talent they wanted, but when Master Romeo found out I was coming to town and looking to build up my business again, he said his friends would be happy to use all the girls I could bring him.

I had a full week's worth of bookings set up with Master Romeo's friends, and girls scheduled to come in from Montreal to fill them, all before I even made it into the country. At the end of my first week in Boston, I already had thousands of dollars in my pocket.

It was a great way to start over. Boston was just a temporary stopover, however. Colonel Ed had told me that he could do for me what he had done for Doug and Sandy's Montreal agency, only in an area of New Jersey that had relatively little competition. I was very interested in that idea, so I decided to look into his offer. And thanks to Master Romeo and his friends, I now had the seed money to do just that and even to start up again full force right away if I decided to.

CHAPTER 9

A Brave New New Jersey

In Boston I got a chance to attend Master Romeo's "high-roller" parties, and that was a trip. I met all the big sharks, guys whose primary goal in life seemed to be to spend as much money as possible. There was one guy who was a real-life 40-Year-Old Virgin. He'd been too busy working on becoming a multimillionaire, I guess, to worry about getting laid when he was still young, but by the time I met him, he was doing his best to make up for lost time. He became an excellent regular customer. I also met a bunch of Montreal Girlfriends who were working the party, and that was useful too. One of those girls was named Mandy, and we became instant friends.

Mandy was a nut job. She had a psychotic boyfriend who was on lithium, and they were always on the verge of killing each other. Her boyfriend was allergic to shellfish, and when she was mad at him, she'd do things that were completely crazy like put pieces of shrimp in his toothpaste. But she made me laugh. After we met, she was always trying to get me to go places and do things with her. She had gotten this idea in her head that after she was done working in Boston she wanted to fly out to San Francisco just to go to this gay club where the guys supposedly jerked off onstage. I had just banked off of the millionaires, so I thought, What the hell? I went with her.

While we were in California together, I told Mandy about

Colonel Ed and his offer to help me start a business in New Jersey. Colonel Ed had told me he had an e-mail list of eight thousand potential clients in a relatively untapped area of northern New Jersey. He said that someone could use his list to set up a small, quiet but lucrative escort agency there without having to place ads in magazines or on the Internet, which could draw unwanted attention. The problem with ads, which were the way I had always started up my businesses before, is that anyone—potential clients, potential employees, as well as potential problems in the way of police or community groups who look for such things—can find them. Even regular people can cause trouble if they make enough noise. But with an e-mail list, I'd have direct and private access to customers so that I could be as discreet as I wanted to be.

It sounded like a great opportunity, which I have a hard time passing up, but I was uncertain about the whole thing. I had never worked in a place like that before. Sure, I had lived with Andre in New Jersey, so I knew the area a little bit, and I'd had my brothels in New York, which isn't very far away, but this would be different. In New Jersey I wouldn't be working out of a big city like I'd done with all my other businesses. This was more like the suburbs, with houses and families. It would have to be a completely different kind of setup than I'd ever had before.

"Maybe he'll let us try it out," Mandy suggested, which was a fantastic idea. She agreed to be my guinea pig. After our trip to San Francisco, we went to test the New Jersey waters and this list of Colonel Ed's.

We decided that the best way to test the effectiveness of Ed's list was to compare it to my old way of starting up a business. First, I used my usual tactic of placing ads in the kinds of magazines and newspapers that I thought locals who might be interested in escort services would see. We advertised that Mandy was in the area for a special visit, one week only, and then sat back and waited to see what would happen.

What happened was not much. We booked maybe four or five appointments over the course of a full week. Mandy met the clients at a local hotel and said they were fine—decent guys and decent tippers—but if I could get only a handful of appointments for the one girl I was running that week, how was I ever going to find enough work to keep several girls busy at a time? I wasn't very hopeful.

A couple weeks later I wrote an e-mail with a similarly worded offer that the Colonel sent out to everyone on his mailing list. We did nothing else but send out that e-mail blast, and, in short, we banked that week. We brought in just over $10,000 in five days, and Mandy walked home with $7,000 in profit. The response was unbelievable. I had to scramble around to find last-minute hotel rooms so that Mandy had a place for all her appointments. (Because I wasn't expecting much, I had booked her a room for only a couple of days.) I even had to turn guys away, and many asked when we'd be coming back. We were both worn out by the end of the week, but I had also made up my mind. This mailing list idea was the way to go. I told Colonel Ed I'd buy his list. The price we agreed on was $50,000.

I thought it was a pretty good deal because I figured I could make that back in just a few months. But it was also more, by far, than I'd ever invested in anything. Besides, I'd done Web sites before but never e-mail lists, and Colonel Ed made it sound hard. He offered to stay on and help me with the technical stuff in exchange for a fee of $500 per girl per week. I went for it. I quickly raised the money I needed, and the Colonel and I became business partners in New Jersey.

One of the first things I did was create an identity for my business. That's when I came up with the name Girlfriend Experience, which tells clients what type of service we offer because most people familiar with the escort industry are familiar with that term. I decided on this because my research into what was already being offered in the area showed that it was all pretty much straight sex, no frills, and not a lot of options. Standing out in that pack was easy. I decided to highlight the fact that we were offering more than just sex; we were offering an erotic *experience*. I figured that would not only set us apart but appeal to the kinds of high-end customers I wanted, the kinds who are professional, stable, and have enough money to use our services regularly.

When we sent out the first e-mail to Colonel Ed's list introducing our new escort agency, I phrased it as if I were offering them admission to an exclusive club. It said, "You have been specially selected to receive a free membership upon approval of your credentials and status. Only qualified applicants are considered for this limited offer." Again, I was appealing to the kinds of customers I wanted, the ones who would be attracted to exclusivity and luxury and who would appreciate, even require, that we be discreet.

I also set up a Web site that customers could go to for more information about us and our girls and included the Web address in the e-mail. After that, I sat back and waited for my phone to ring. It rang almost immediately.

I didn't bother to check a guy out until he called to set up an appointment. But once he did call, he wasn't allowed to go any further until he gave me some basic biographical information: his name, where he worked, his office phone, his home phone. I often had to coax the information out of people, but I didn't mind that. I'd just tell them, "Listen, sweetie, I know this makes you uncomfortable, but it's really best for all of us. You wouldn't want me to send you a girl I hadn't checked out beforehand, would you? Everyone has to be screened or none of us are safe. Besides, once you're cleared, I won't hang on to your information," which was mostly true; since I have a good memory, I keep most of it, except for the e-mail addresses, in my head. Then I'd continue: "I don't want your personal information exposed any more than you do." I was always happy to give a new guy that speech, and it nearly always worked. In fact, the more hesitant a guy was to give me his personal information, the better I felt about him. I've turned down customers just because they sounded too eager on the phone.

Once I had a guy's info, I'd tell him I would call him back after he'd been fully screened and okayed. It sounded very official, but I would actually begin the process the same place you probably would, by simply Googling him. I would also call his office to verify that he actually worked there. Sometimes I called home and talked to his wife while pretending to be a telemarketer. The kinds of questions I asked depended on what sort of feeling I got about a person, but I kept asking until I felt comfortable. And if I didn't feel comfortable, then I just never called him back.

If you are accepted as a client, it typically works like this: You can go to our Web site and check out the photos of the girls who are working that week along with their basic stats: height, weight, measurements, ethnicity, hair and eye color, and, often, what their pubic hair looks like (as in "completely bald," "natural," "landing strip"). Then, of course, there are the personality profiles, which are a little bit of fiction. I create the stories myself and consider it one of my best talents. None of the girls use their real names, of course, so we make up a stage name for each of them and then create a personality from there.

Some of them are teachers who know how to take control of any situation. Others are foreigners with sexy accents who are new to this country and perhaps a bit lost and in need of help. Some are sweet and innocent students who are looking to be schooled. We've had acrobats and masseuses, nurses and mommies, librarians and all sorts of others. Other times, we just offer a particularly juicy description of a girl's best assets, particularly for our regular girls, like this profile of Ginny from Nevada:

Back by popular demand, Ginny of Nevada is visiting the Northern New Jersey area! For those who have not yet had the pleasure of meeting this beautiful *Vixen,* she is an absolute charmer and a natural to the Girlfriend Experience. As a well-known and reputable provider, she will accommodate you with genuine enthusiasm, pleasuring you with a complete, never rushed, and oh-so-amazingly romantic experience. Afterward, you'll feel like you've just woken up from a dream.

Ginny is 5'9", 130 lbs, 36D, with long silky dark hair and bright blue eyes. Her body is firm and athletic with incredible curves in just the right places. She complements her *Perfect* proportions and model features with such an eager need to please. She is willing and wanting to lose all inhibitions and to attend to your every wish or *Desire* . . . perhaps even show you another meaning of the word.

Once you've found the girl you want, you simply call or e-mail for an appointment. There is a Web form right on our site that you can use to book appointments. There is even a credit card form that our most trusted customers can use if they don't want to pay cash. Most men prefer to call, however. (All our clients have my personal cell phone number.) My guys are looking for instant gratification, and waiting around for an e-mail reply just isn't as much fun as talking to me on the phone. Still, if they can't get in touch with me, because I don't work twenty-four hours a day, they have some backup options, which usually makes them feel better.

We operate on a standard two-call system, which means that when you call the agency for an appointment, you'll get the name of and directions to the hotel where the meeting will take place but not the room number. To get the room number, you have to call a second time when you arrive at the hotel and let us know that you're ready. Then, I call the girl to make sure she's ready. You have to remember that we usually book clients back-to-back if we can, so I call the girl to make sure her last appointment is finished, that the guy has left the room, and that she has had a chance to tidy up before you arrive. There's nothing worse than a client arriving at the door and seeing the previous customer walking out. That can really kill the mood. Only after the girl has given me the okay do I give the next client the room number and send him up. That's when the clock starts.

I don't know exactly what happens after that since I'm never around, and frankly, I don't want to know. Once they're in a room together, I leave it up to the girls and the clients to figure things out as much as possible. Of course, I have my rules, which are spelled out for all the girls in my employee handbook, but I know they aren't always followed to the letter. The girls aren't supposed to do drugs when they're working, for example, but I know it happens all the time. In fact, I offer this bit of advice to all the clients of one girl who works for me semi-regularly: "I have a little secret for you about this particular girl. If you don't mind the smell, let her smoke a joint before you start. You'll have a much better time, I guarantee it." The clients, without exception, have appreciated that tidbit.

My official policy is that everyone must follow all the rules. In reality, however, drugs are more of a don't ask, don't tell kind of thing, as long as they're controlled. If I don't get any complaints, then I don't care. But if a girl overdoes it and a customer lets me know that she passed out or was acting crazy or partook in something in front of him that made him uncomfortable, I fire her for getting out of line.

I can fire girls when I need to because I have a large pool of girls to draw from. In fact, I try to use different ones every week. Most of my girls don't live in the area but instead fly in from wherever they live—Florida, California, Canada, sometimes Europe—and stay in the hotel where they're working for a week, sometimes two at a time.

There are two good reasons for using out-of-town talent. First, using a different set of girls—girls who live all over the country, sometimes the world—each week makes it much harder for anyone to bust my agency, because it's much more difficult to use a girl to get inside my organization and get to me. Second, variety is the spice of life. From a marketing perspective, every time a new girl comes in from somewhere, I've got a reason to send out an e-mail blast advertising my new merchandise. Besides, I have clients who use our service on a regular basis, as often as once or twice a week, and if I offered them the same girls week after week after week, they'd soon get bored with us.

"Donations" are $300 to $350 an hour for experienced girls, as I've said before, but when I get a new girl who needs some experience, I will often offer her services for $250 an hour until she's built up a reputation. I have lots of clients who are happy to break someone in at a discounted price and then report back to me on whether she's worth keeping. We also run specials on the Web site, for Valentine's Day, for example, and give clients a break on their birthdays along with "a nice complimentary bottle of red or white wine or some bubbly to celebrate your special occasion!" Of course, I have several clients who claim it's their birthday every few months, so I make sure to note in the birthday special announcement that "IDs will be inspected on your arrival." We offer special lunch-hour half hours at a lesser rate for guys who are crunched for time but want to get in a quickie before getting back to work. We offer $50 discounts for referring a friend to our service, a $500 discount for recommending a qualified entertainer. I also have a "frequent flier" program for our best customers.

In addition to accepting donations, I'm a big believer in barter theory. On my site I say it this way: "Are you interested in bartering with us? Are you an accountant? A computer tech? Car mechanic? Doctor? Lawyer? Internet security specialist? Health insurance agent? (I'm looking to get medical and dental coverage for all of my girls.) We may be able to work out a special arrangement with you!"

I like doing business this way because it allows me to get goods and services without having my name attached or recorded. I've gotten a new Mercedes, a couple of apartments, all my legal work done, and some of my Web work, not to mention some badly needed medications from a pharmaceutical rep and even therapy, all by trading free or discounted appointments for what I wanted or needed.

I allow my girls to do the same and make arrangements with clients for what they need, but I do that only with the girls I know well and trust. If you work for me, you have to earn privileges by being a good employee. Before a girl can work for me, she has to sign a contract and agree to the rules. All this is explained to her up-front. In fact, the first thing I do when anyone calls me looking for a job is send over the employee handbook. Many potential employees drop out after reading my rules, but that's fine with me. Those who are still interested are more likely to be professionals who are good at their jobs.

Of course girls in this business aren't always the professional types, so I have to check up on them as best I can. Take Serena, for example. She was an Eastern European model who was referred to me by a client. The agency she was working for at the time was one of those $1,500-an-hour outfits in New York City, but she wasn't getting enough work there, so despite the drastic pay cut, she decided to come work for me. At first, she wanted me to charge more for her, to sell her as a special, premium-priced offering, but I told her it was my policy not to treat one girl like she was worth more than any of the others. (I wasn't always like that; that's a business principle I had to learn.) My philosophy is that there is somebody for everyone out there and so every girl costs roughly the same, even the fat ones or the older ones or the flat-chested ones or ones who aren't that pretty. Some of my top earners over the years would surprise you—like Bette, who has kind of a pig nose, or Jill, who is rounder than most—but they always get excellent reviews from customers for their uninhibited behavior. If you saw girls like them across the room, you wouldn't be all that impressed, but behind closed doors, they're good at what they do. Serena finally agreed to my terms, and so I put her to work.

Serena was an easy sell. Based on her pictures and her pedigree, lots of guys were anxious to get an appointment with her. But just like with anything else you'd buy at a severely discounted rate, there was reason to be suspicious.

Her first week she did extremely well. We filled up every available hour with appointments, close to three dozen in all. She was very happy with the money she made, and so was I, so I booked her in for another week of work about a month later.

By that time, however, her reviews had come out, and they were dismal, some of the worst I'd ever seen. The next time she came around, she booked about half as many appointments. At that point, I hadn't caught on to what was happening yet, so, figuring it was just a fluke, I had her back for a third time. By then, word had spread far and wide, and I booked three appointments for her all week. I've never had anyone do so badly before or since. I couldn't even give her away to a regular client who had seen her once before and felt he deserved a refund.

Finally I asked that client if he would confide in me about the problem. Well, when the floodgates opened, he couldn't say enough bad things about her.

"First of all," he said, "she looked nothing like her pictures, which is not to say that she wasn't reasonably attractive, but when you're expecting one thing and something else answers the door, it can definitely kill the mood. It would have been better if she had just taken new pictures and shown herself as she really is now instead of using outdated and airbrushed model pictures, which just didn't represent her at all. Second, and this was even worse, the place was disgusting. I don't think she did a thing to clean up all day, and the last thing I wanted to be thinking about was all the other guys who had been in that room before me. But I couldn't help it. It was so obvious. The evidence was all over the place. Third, she wasn't very well groomed. Being European, I guess she's more comfortable with body hair and all that, but if you ask me, the full bush—hairy pits thing went out of style in the seventies! And finally, her service was horrible. She didn't seem to be having fun. She didn't talk much. It was like, let's do this and get it over with. I don't need to pay for attitude like that. I can get that at home!"

I thanked my client and gave him a discount on his next appointment in exchange for his honesty. And then, since she had violated a whole bunch of my rules and was basically offering clients the exact opposite of the girlfriend experience, I told the $1,500-an-hour girl she could never work for me again.

I worked hard in the beginning, but the payoff was worth it. I made good money from the very start. Since I was living just across the water, I went into Manhattan a lot when I wanted to play and let off steam. I started dating this boy named Austin, who was a traveling stripper and sometimes worked at The Gaiety, the notorious male strip club in Times Square that was featured in Madonna's *Sex* book. He was a gorgeous boy with the prettiest eyes I've ever seen. Our relationship didn't last long, but my relationships with some of his friends did. He hung out with this model-esque group of guys who were a lot of fun. One of them, Jano, lived in Miami, and somehow we got it in our heads that I should move down there too.

The business was working out well in New Jersey, so I wanted to keep it going but I also wanted a change of scenery. I talked to Colonel Ed about it, and he told me to go ahead. This was a new era for me business-wise, when everything was done remotely, via Internet or cell phone, anyway. There was no reason, as the Colonel pointed out, that I couldn't do exactly what I was doing already, only from the beach in Florida.

I was psyched that I didn't have to be chained to my desk. I found a phenomenal apartment in Miami that I was dying to live in, but I somehow had to convince the managers of the apartment complex that I could pay the rent even though I didn't have a credit history or anything like that. I finally decided to send them nine months of receipts from the upscale hotel I'd been living in in New Jersey, and they took that as proof enough that I'd be a responsible tenant.

I also made a deal with Jano. He was always having money problems, so I told him he could be my roommate if he would lease a car we both could use. (I hadn't had a license since my purse was stolen when I was living in Montreal, and without one, I couldn't lease a car myself.) I guess I was far too trusting then about letting people into my life and business. In the end, both Jano and the Colonel screwed me.

It all started when I got pulled over for running a stop sign. It shouldn't have been that big of a deal, but when I finally went down to the courthouse to pay the ticket some time later, I found out that I was too late. If you don't pay your tickets in Florida within a certain number of days, then you have to straighten things out directly with the police.

So then I went down to the police station, where they looked me up and found out that I had a seven-year-old warrant out for my arrest in New Jersey. It was just this stupid thing that happened to me when I was in Atlantic City after Tito was murdered. I had been leasing a car and was late on one payment (not surprising with everything that was going on in my life then), so the car company had reported it stolen. I was exhausted from driving one night and pulled over at a hotel where all I wanted to do was relax in the Jacuzzi and then go to bed. When I got back to my room after taking a dip, the police were banging on my door. They'd seen the car in the parking lot and run the license plate. Then they came into my room and went through everything. In the bathroom they found a tiny little vial with just traces of cocaine, which must have been left there by the room's previous occupant. It really wasn't mine. I hadn't even unpacked yet. Still, the car charge was dropped, but the possession charge stuck, so I was supposed to return to court some time later for a hearing. I never showed, which is why they issued a warrant for my arrest. And I guess arrest warrants, even for small things, never go away, not even after seven years.

I wasn't all that worried at first, just annoyed that this had happened when things were going so well for me business-wise, and personally too, since I loved living in Florida. Talk about your past sneaking up on you. I figured either Jano or the Colonel would come to my rescue and bail me out. I waited and waited, but they never came. Instead they decided to leave me there and take over my business.

I was the one who had all the connections with girls from all over, who I'd bring in for a week or two at a time to fill appointments. And I was the one who'd been building relationships with the clients on Colonel Ed's list so that they would trust us. And I had been generous to both those guys. I had already started to figure out that Colonel Ed was getting much more than he deserved. I had befriended this computer genius in Miami, and he had shown me how easy it is to manage mailing lists and send out e-mail blasts, which was all the Colonel was doing in exchange for his ongoing fee. He had convinced me it was such complicated work that I needed him to stay on to help me with it. Even after I found out that that was bullshit, I kept working with him.

Jano was even worse. To try to help him get on his feet so he could make some money of his own and get out of my apartment, I had built up a male escort service in Miami for him to run. I made him this really hot Web site, but he couldn't handle the work. I ended up running both businesses while he mooched off me. I was making sick money, and I developed an amazing collection of Louis Vuitton handbags during that period, but it was also exhausting and I was going out of my mind by the time I got arrested.

All in all, it took two whole months before I got out and could rescue my business. It took so long because I was extradited to New Jersey, which was an excruciatingly slow process. When I finally got there, I was eventually let out on probation since the charge was from so long ago and it had been just a small amount of drugs. But by that point, the damage was done.

The first thing I did when I was let out was go down to Miami to find out where all my stuff was. Jano and his girlfriend (who, I had heard, moved into my apartment when I wasn't there) had split, and there was practically nothing left in the place. I called 911 as soon as I got there, and the police found out that some of my stuff had been stashed with a neighbor. I got back my computers and some of my furniture, but all my good clothes were gone, not to mention my Louis Vuitton collection.

I flew back to New Jersey with my tail between my legs. To make matters worse, I'd gained a lot of weight—about forty pounds—while I was in jail, so I was feeling really bad about the way I looked. I started to feel better, however, when I began look-ing into taking back my agency. I found out that Jano and Colonel Ed had done such a bad job while I was gone that everyone was happy to have me back. They had booked an appointment for Mandy, for example, with a serial mugger who was known for slashing people up. He didn't hurt her, but he did tie her up and steal all her money and her Rolex. I was more than a little pissed at her for working for those guys while I was in jail, but I played on her guilt to get her to blow them off and work for me instead. And the clients I talked to were just as dissatisfied with the service they'd been getting.

I set everything up for a killer week before I announced my return. I brought in a bunch of girls from Montreal and booked hotels for all of them. Jano hadn't thought to erase all my contacts from my computers when he left them behind, so I still knew how to get in touch with the original list. I sent out a mass e-mail to clients, girls, friends, everyone. The subject line read: "HOSTILE TAKEOVER!!!"

It wasn't hard to take my agency back after that. Jano dropped off the face of the earth, probably afraid of what I'd do to him if I found him. And Colonel Ed ended up getting arrested for something else. Business was better than ever after that, and finally, it was entirely on my terms.

The second time around I decided I should run my business in New Jersey from New Jersey and by myself from then on. Thanks to my computer nerd friend, I had learned a few tricks, and I began testing out what I could do to make the list I'd bought from the Colonel even better. The first thing I did was plant ads on free sites, local Craigslist-type places, using stock pictures of half-naked girls. After that I sent an e-mail to everyone on the list offering them free access if they just entered their full names, some other basic information, and confirmed their e-mail addresses. Then I sat back and waited for guys to contact me. Using the information I received as a result, I began cleaning up the list by eliminating duplicate contacts, addresses that were bounced back, and anyone who responded with a request to unsubscribe.

I have used the same stock-photo trick to build up my list on occasion too. The problem is, it can take a really long time and a lot of effort to keep posting fake ads in places where potential customers will see them and wait for them to respond. That's why I still think, despite everything that happened with the Colonel, that buying that list from him was a good investment. And because I've done so much work on it over the years, I now consider it my most valuable asset.

I have pared down the Colonel's original list from eight thousand addresses to a targeted e-mail list of about two thousand men in the

New Jersey area, all of whom have been carefully and methodically checked out by me personally and who I know are interested in the services I offer. Besides using the planted ad trick, I have added to the list over the years through referrals and personal contacts, but that initial list still accounts for the majority of my customers. By now I know these guys' habits, what they're looking for, and how often they come looking for it. I know that they're all legitimate customers, not cops (except for the cops who have been cleared to use our services). I also know what they do, where they work, if they're married (most of them are), if they have kids (most of them do), and, in many cases, even more personal things, like how good their marriages are and how happy they are with their jobs. (Guys often like to chat when they call me.) Having that information makes me feel much more calm and secure about the business I'm in. The best clients are those with the most to lose: they don't want anyone to find out about my business any more than I do.

I started out in New Jersey more than six years ago, but my business has always worked pretty much the same way, although my Web site has gotten more sophisticated and I've had a chance to try out all kinds of different marketing techniques to see what works. It didn't take long to build up a steady stream of work, which has kept me busy to maximum capacity ever since. More often than not, I have more work than I can handle, and I've had to learn how to say no, how to take days off, and how to just let the phone ring without answering it. That last one is still hard for me.

One of the most interesting things about how the business has changed over the years is that it has all gotten a lot more transparent. While I may be able to feel more secure about what I do because of modern technology and how it allows me to do my entire job behind closed doors, I'm also held to a higher standard. Thanks to those very popular review sites, where customers share information about their experiences, clients know much more than ever even before they even get around to calling us.

The rip-off agency I ran in Baltimore could not happen, not for long anyway, in today's environment because of these sites. Guys would be able to read about how we didn't deliver on the promise (or *implied* promise) of sex, and they just wouldn't call us, simple as that. Men looking in the yellow pages, as they did back then, didn't know anything more than what you wanted them to know, but today anyone with enough money to afford our service also has a computer, and he can look up each girl on the review sites. All the truly professional escorts can be found there, and guys do check them regularly, so if a girl wants her career to continue, she has to keep her ratings up. And the practice is good for us too. It helps me monitor what's going on with my girls, which is important since I'm never actually in the room with them when they're working. Besides, the better her reviews, the more I can charge for a girl (I often charge a premium for "perfect 10" girls). I even show up in the reviews sometimes, with guys critiquing my phone manner. (They often mention my sweet and sultry voice.) Sometimes guys like to get poetic with their descriptions of their encounters or even give play-by-plays, like the review in the next paragraph. Generally speaking, however, guys have less to say when they are satisfied. A typical glowing review can be something like "Attitude: Sweet; Appearance: Hot; Recommended: Yes; Price: $300." But if a customer feels he's been screwed over in some way, boy do we hear about it.

Here's a review that was posted one evening when I was having phone trouble and the girl who was working was fighting off a cold:

> When I called to set up the appointment, I told [the agent] I might be late and she said that was fine, she'd only charge me for a ½ hour if that's all I was there for. I was thinking, cool.
>
> But then I got to the spot on time and called the number. I got some message saying my call could not be completed. I waited 10

minutes, called back, same issue. Waited another ten, same thing. At 8:45, fifteen minutes after my appointment was supposed to start, I tried sending an email from my blackberry saying I couldn't get through on her phone. She called me back five minutes later and gave me the room number. I thought, ok, fine. I ran upstairs, told [the girl] I would only need a half hour, gave her the donation, and jumped in the shower.

When I got out, [the girl] said, "Please call the agency and ask the rate because I was told you were paying for a full hour and I don't want to get stuck paying the extra." I tried calling. I couldn't get through. Finally she said we could call again after the session.

Onto the session. [The girl], as previously reported, has very well done implants which feel terrific and respond wonderfully. I went to work on them and here's the 1st snag—BO :(. Her armpits smelled a bit, which was a turn off. I kind of nudged her down for some BBBJ [bare back blow job] and she complied. As she was going to town, I started feeling her legs and they were hairy. WTF?!

She gave nice BBBJ—hands, no hands, dt [deep throat], just the head, a really good mix—but when I moved her to mish [missionary position], the armpit smell came back. At this point, I asked if she could finish with her mouth. She said ok.

I can't say I was happy about the review, but it was fair. It wasn't our best night. We made it up to him, though.

It's really the World Wide Web, and not the law, that has brought some sort of order and regulation to this industry. And to tell you the truth, I prefer it the way it works now. Terms like *professionalism, reliability, pride in your work* weren't ever used when I first started out, but now I don't know how you could possibly run a business without these principles.

CHAPTER 10

Intimate (Business) Relations

Now that I've established a successful and lucrative business, my entire frame of mind is geared toward minimizing my personal risk. That's why I do my best never to meet clients or employees in person. (Except for those I already know, of course. I still bring in lots of girls who I've worked with before in various places, and who are friends of mine.) I'm perfectly accessible by phone, e-mail, or through my Web site, but there is really no reason for them to know me, know where I work, or even know my real name. I go by a stage name too, just like my girls.

Not only is this safer for me but it also adds to the mystique. When I've met my ladies in the past, they've often been shocked by how young I am. Between that and my sweet and friendly personality, they start to see me in a different light, more as a friend and someone to hang out with than as a boss. That's when they start slipping. They think I'll understand if they're late or if they want to go tanning during business hours and I can't reach them. They think I want to listen to them complain about their boyfriends or about clients for silly reasons because, after all, I'm like a friend to them. But I don't understand and I don't want to listen. What I care about is working hard and making money. Keeping my distance from people is the best way to do that. It's not personal, it's business.

The separation between church and state, so to speak, was so important to me that my best friend, Mandy, and I had to decide when I set up shop in New Jersey whether we were going to be friends or colleagues. I knew we couldn't do both, because we knew each other too well. We chose to be friends. She doesn't work for me anymore, but she still visits sometimes.

As the boss, I can break my own rules if I want to, but I've found that when I do, I often get into trouble. Tracey, stage name Sindy, was one of my most extreme examples of getting too close to a girl. I met her when I was in Montreal, where she worked for a pimp-run agency that I continued to trade girls with after I set up in New Jersey. It's something I do now and then with this and other agencies whenever I need to bring in fresh meat. (I prefer ones that aren't run by pimps, but the business comes first; I do what I need to do to keep my customers happy.) That's how Sindy came to be working for me one week in New Jersey.

Sindy's pimp was a real dick, and I felt sorry for her—my first mistake. She was sweet and pretty, and we had gotten along when I knew her in Montreal, even though I didn't know her well. But I liked her, so one day when she started crying, I made another mistake—I asked her what was wrong.

She told me she was crying because she had recently, finally, paid off her pimp so she could go out on her own, but then he changed the deal on her. When she began working for him, he made her believe she owed him, not just a percentage of her income but also a flat payment of some ridiculous amount for getting her started, if you can believe that. Somehow she managed to pay him the money, but he was still insisting that she give him a cut of whatever she made, whether he booked the appointment for her or not. I told you that pimps think they own their girls, and that's how this guy saw Sindy, as someone he'd own for as long as he felt like it—forever if that's what he wanted.

I hated to see this because I know what it's like to be taken advantage of by pimps. I thought of Julio and the guy Natasha had run off with and others whose paths I had, unfortunately, crossed over the years. Part of my problem was that I love to stick it to guys like that, who think they can take advantage of women just because they're women. Against my better judgment, I told Sindy that if she wanted to get away from her pimp, she shouldn't go home. She should stay in New Jersey and continue working for me. And that's what she did.

A lot of people would say I did the right thing, but business is business, and in most cases there are reasons why a girl is stuck in a situation as bad as hers. Sindy was not the kind of person who knew how to make it on her own, and I quickly realized that what she really wanted was not to get away from pimps altogether but just to get a new one, who would be nicer to her and pay her more money. She needed someone who was going to take control of her life and tell her what to do. Unfortunately for her, "nice" pimps don't really exist, and being a caretaker for my girls is not part of my job description.

Taking Sindy's side cost me a very successful work relationship. Her pimp obviously didn't appreciate that I helped his girl leave him, and we no longer traded talent after that. The worst part of it all was that I sacrificed that relationship just to get stuck with another needy girl.

Sindy was like a child, always late or disappearing for days at a time. When she managed to make it to work, she was amazing and guys loved her, but in order to get her to show up, I had to become her mother, her best friend, her caretaker, and her psychiatrist.

She'd go on drug binges and take off with guys she didn't even know, so I would have to stop whatever I was doing and go find her before she got herself into any serious trouble. She didn't really have any friends around, so I felt responsible for her. When she wasn't on drugs she talked about committing suicide, which made me feel like I needed to keep watch over her. One of my agency's hard-and-fast rules is that girls *must* practice safe sex, no exceptions. Sindy did manage to follow that rule when she was on appointments, probably thanks to her clients rather than her own will, but when she was off the clock, she had unsafe partner after unsafe partner.

That was too much for me. The last thing I wanted was to have to call up my clients to tell them that the girl they saw last week just tested positive for HIV. That happened to me once before, when I was in Montreal. I left too many of those decisions up to the girls and their customers back then, until I found out that one of my former employees had gotten really sick. One of her former clients had been a good friend of mine, and giving him the news was one of the worst moments in my whole life.

Unfortunately, not even I can stop caring about someone just like that. I had to fire Sindy, and the only way I could do it was if I knew she had somewhere to go. When she was with me and on her game, she had been making close to $10,000 a month, but somehow she'd managed to blow all that money. I gave her $2,500, sent her home to her family, and took it all as a lesson. I'm no shrink—I can't help a girl with that many problems, no matter how much I may want to. I need to stick to what I'm good at. I've heard that Sindy is back with the same pimp in Montreal, which doesn't surprise me at all. Sometimes you're just lucky to get a girl like that out of your life before she can cause too much damage.

Sindy never paid that $2,500 back to me, but I'm not even going to bother trying to get the money from her, which is not like me at all. Another one of my rules is that if you owe me money, then you owe me money, and you'd better pay it back one way or another. In Sindy's case, though, I wrote it off as a gift. It was guilt money really. I couldn't help her, so I paid her off to get her off my hands. If there hadn't been those special circumstances, however, it would have been a much bigger problem between us.

Money is the thing my girls and I fight over the most by far: they're late with their payments or they forget how much they owe me or they pay me the wrong amount because they can't count. Sometimes it's an honest mistake—after all, most of them will never be confused with rocket scientists—but sometimes it's not. The problem is, I often don't know which it is, and I can't completely trust any of the girls who work for me. Most girls in this industry are not the type to think ahead, especially when it comes to money. They get $1,000 in their pockets and they act like they're set forever.

Take, for example, Kristi, stage name Ginger, who had worked for me a bunch of times and been nothing but professional. Ginger is a tall blond bombshell with 36DD breasts who looks like a porn star. In fact, she has done some movie work before. She has probably been working for ten years, and why not? She still looks great, and her reviews are always perfect tens. You'd think I'd be able to rely on a girl like that. But even she tried to screw me once.

Ginger had been meeting clients in the hotel room I got for her all week and had paid my assistants faithfully every night when they came around to collect my share. That is, until the end of the week, on her very last day in town. That's when she decided not to wait around for my assistant, taking off instead with all the cash from that day.

I'm not an unreasonable person. Maybe there was a reason why she had to leave early. Maybe there was a reason why she needed some extra cash that day. If she had bothered to call and tell me what was up, I would have worked something out with her. But Ginger just disappeared with $1,000 of my money.

Still, I didn't freak out. I called and left her a message saying we had some settling up to do. She never called me back. I called her once a month after that and left the same message: "You know you owe me some money and we have to figure out a way to settle up." Each time, nothing. That went on for a year and a half before I did anything about it. I always give girls a decent amount of time to make things right. It's the only fair thing to do.

I had heard through the grapevine that Ginger was working for another agency in the area, so one day, after she hadn't returned my call again, I had a guy friend of mine call the other agency to make an appointment with her. The plan was this: He would pretend to be a client looking for the last appointment of the day, but when he showed up at her hotel room, he'd rob her instead. And that's exactly what my friend did. He's a big guy, a former bouncer at a club, and he's licensed to carry a firearm. He also brought along a friend to help. They didn't hurt her, but two big guys with guns will definitely scare a girl.

The guys were very professional. They got to Ginger's room, gathered up all the money she'd made that day, counted it, and then, per my instructions, put one-third of it back on the bedside table. That was the cut for the agency she was working for. My issue was with Ginger alone, and leaving the agency's money behind would make it clear that I wasn't interested in screwing them, just the girl. (I also called the agency to let them know this in case Ginger decided to take off with their money too.) Then, on their way out, the guys made sure Ginger understood why this was happening. "If you had settled your debts, this never would have happened to you," the bouncer told her. I'm sure she got the point.

The guys brought me my $1,000 and kept the rest for themselves as payment for their services. I wasn't looking to make money off of this, just to get what I was owed and settle the score. The guys got about $1,500 to share for a half an hour of work.

It's not like I go straight to that kind of tactic. Like I said, it had been over a year and I had given her all sorts of chances. She could have paid me in installments, she could have worked it off, but one way or another she had to pay. She didn't take me up on any of my offers, so she left me with no choice.

I know $1,000 is not a lot of money, but it's not the amount that matters. Word gets around. If one girl gets away with stealing from you, the others eventually hear about it and you have a nasty trend on your hands. So I can't let those things stand, not for any amount. Especially me. Being a young woman in this business has its advantages, but it has its drawbacks too, one of which is that people are more likely to think they can get away with shit. The girls should know better by now, and they should know that we will see each other again. We live and work in a pretty small world. I want all my girls, if they are considering doing what Ginger did, to think that I have a long memory and I will catch up with them eventually, so what's the point? Do you want to be watching your back for the rest of your life because you owe someone a measly $1,000? Unfortunately, a lot of the girls aren't that smart. If they were, they'd do what I do instead of what they do.

None of my girls could ever accuse me of not being fair. I never try to steal from them. I don't even charge interest when they're late in paying me. I just want what I'm owed. And Ginger learned her lesson. She was back working for me a few months later, and she hasn't misbehaved since.

I wish I could say that, once I made an example out of Ginger, that kind of thing never happened again. But it has happened again, and it will continue to happen. Girls are just like that.

Other tactics I've used to get even with girls and encourage them to settle their debts with me: calling up a husband or boyfriend to tell him what his precious lady really does with her spare time; burning a CD of a girl's promotional pictures to send to her family; and putting a notice on my Web site under a girl's pictures, along with her real name, for all our clients and whoever else visits the site to see, saying: "This girl's services won't be available until she pays back the money she owes us. Until then, her pictures and this notice will remain on our site."

As for my clients, most of them are hardworking professionals like doctors (the most common profession to hire my girls by far), lawyers, executives, and business owners (with one exception: our UPS delivery boy; how he affords to come by as often as he does, I'm not quite sure). They all have cash to spare and things to lose, which is just as important as the money, because it helps keep me and my business safe. And they need me as much as I need them. Even though a lot of the smarter girls market themselves on the Internet these days, most upscale clients don't really have time to troll the Web looking for what they want. And even if they did, they don't like giving out their personal information to a different girl every week. They want to do this safely too, and if they go through me, someone they know, they can choose from a variety of girls while having to trust only one person with their phone and credit card numbers. My girls don't even need to know a client's real name unless he tells it to them himself.

I try to live by the old rule "The customer is always right," except that sometimes he isn't. That's true even for my guys, who are, for the most part, a pretty nice bunch. But just because a guy looks like an upstanding citizen during the day doesn't mean he is one. We get all kinds of personality types calling us. "Different strokes for different folks" is what I say, and as long as they abide by the terms of our deal and behave themselves, I don't judge them (not in front of them anyway).

There was this one guy, for example, who never wanted to have sex. He just wanted someone to treat him like a baby, literally. He'd bring along a bottle, pacifier, and adult-size diapers, and the girl was supposed to feed, burp, and change him. Whatever. He was too out there for a couple of my girls, but most didn't really mind. It was a pretty easy hour for them. Babies, after all, mostly just lie there.

He wasn't the only one who asked for things other than sex. I had another client from New York who also brought along his own props. In his case, they were a long plastic tube and a small rodent. He had the girl stick the lubed-up tube in his ass, put the gerbil, or whatever it was, inside, and then wait for it to crawl upward. Once it had, she pulled out the tube, and the poor thing scratched around in his ass until it eventually suffocated. But that wasn't what excited this guy the most. What he really looked forward to was when the girl took him to the hospital afterward to have the rodent removed. He had specified in advance that she wear her sluttiest stripper wear, so that when they arrived at the emergency room, there was no doubt about her profession. And then he couldn't wait to tell everyone that there was "something stuck up my butt." It was the humiliation that really got him off.

One of my all-time best clients has never once had sex with my girls, and he's hired a lot of them. He's in the insurance business and way into S&M, as a stress release I think. He'll sometimes hire a bunch of girls at once, and, since he's not married, they often go to his house. Once he went to the store and bought bags and bags of sex toys, enough to practically fill a whole room. When the girls arrived, they spent the first hour just unwrapping the toys and putting batteries in the ones that needed them. Easy money. He's got tons of cash and a huge house, including a full basketball court. Another time he tied a girl upside down to the post under his basketball net. Normally I'd say no to a request like that because someone could get hurt, but this guy was such a sweetheart and such a big tipper that all the girls loved working for him. And since he was a regular, I knew I could trust him.

I don't blame a guy for being freaky, I just make sure my girls know what they're getting into. But if any client ever mistreats any of my girls—if he tries to hurt her or threatens her or even if he's just disrespectful in the way he talks to her—I blacklist him right away. Depending on the circumstances, I may even post what happened on one of the public review sites so everyone else knows to be wary of the guy as well. Like I said, these sites protect all parties.

I would post a warning only if a guy gets violent or out of control or steals from a girl or threatens her. If he "forgets" to pay, well, that's a different kind of problem. That's really the girl's responsibility. She is supposed to collect her donation up-front, and if a guy doesn't pay, then he gets no play. If a girl forgets to ask for the money, then it's her fault. In those situations I tell the girl she has to work it out on her own, which usually means she ends up eating the loss and pays me my share out of her own pocket. But that's okay. It helps her remember the procedures the next time around.

I once had a regular client who was the head of a big technology company and liked to tell girls exactly what to do. I mean *exactly,* down to the smallest details. He had to be in charge of everything, telling a girl where to put her hand, then what to say, then when to move and how.

I didn't think that was a big deal, but then I started to hear some more disturbing stories about him. He asked a few girls I knew to come along with him while he vacationed on his yacht one summer. He made his own deal with the girls so I wasn't responsible, but I was still disturbed by what they told me. At first they were psyched and jumped at the chance without thinking it through. Personally, I would have been really concerned about being on a boat with a guy I barely knew, since I couldn't turn around and go home whenever I wanted to. And just as I thought, as soon as they got out onto the open water, he wouldn't let them out of his sight. He treated them like dogs, telling them when to sit, when to eat, when to sleep, what to wear. It sounded like a nightmare.

One of the girls called me crying from a hotel in the Bahamas, where they had stopped for the night. She'd gone with him thinking it would be a big party on a big boat, but she felt like a hostage.

"Get your own room and then get on the first plane out of there in the morning," I told her. "And call the police if he gives you any problems." But she didn't want to do that because she didn't want to spend her own money to get home. Stupid. As far as I'm concerned, whatever happened to her after that was as much her fault as it was his.

Still, the guy was an asshole, and I thought that was enough to blacklist him from my service. Truthfully, I thought the baby man was an asshole too, but he's harmless, so I still have him as a client to this day.

CHAPTER 11

Love and Karma

I try to tell myself that I don't need anyone. Business works better that way, when I'm on my own with no attachments and no liabilities. But no matter what I do, I always find myself back in the same situation time and time again. I know it's smarter for me to be alone, but there's a strong part of me that just doesn't want to be. And the worst part is that, the older I get, the stronger that piece of myself seems to become.

When I started my agency in New Jersey, Philippe, my soul mate from Montreal, would still call me sometimes. Then one day my old hairdresser from Montreal, who I always stayed in touch with, told me that Philippe had gotten married. He knew because he had fixed Philippe's wife's hair for the wedding. It sounded like Philippe had done it for the papers, because he was an immigrant and wanted to stay in Canada, but still, my heart broke. I didn't have sex for an entire year after I found out.

Of course, my year as a born-again virgin included the time I was in jail for two months and gained all that weight. I wasn't having sex in jail, obviously, and then the extra weight and all the work I had to do to take my agency back helped keep me chaste. I did date like a fiend, however, after my business in New Jersey was back on track. But most of the guys didn't stick around too long when they found out that the madam didn't put out.

I finally started working out with a trainer and took up boxing to get me back to my "fighting weight." Eventually, I fell in love again. His name was Mark, and we met through a mutual friend. He was a chef at a hotel restaurant and very successful. We moved in together into an apartment in New Jersey, we went on vacation together, we even bought a dog together—my little pug, Max. Mark accepted me for who I was and what I did. In the end, however, I didn't leave Mark. I made him leave me. I found out from a friend of his that he had been offered a great job in another city but had turned it down because of what it would do to our relationship. Before this it had always been my boyfriends who held me back, not the other way around. I couldn't be responsible for that, so as much as it killed me, I had to let him go.

I should have stuck with the vow of chastity that had been working for me before I met Mark. Because after Mark, my love life just went downhill. I was in a dark dance club in New York one night when Freddie shined a flashlight on me and gave me a huge smile. That's how we met. At least that's how I met him. He met me about an hour later, after the drugs wore off and he came out of his K-hole.

Freddie was the kind of person who was impossible to miss, even without his flashlight. He was tall, dark, and lean. Not classically good-looking, but he had an interesting face and interesting tattoos, and he was fit. I later learned that he worked out like it was his second job, and it was his physicality that first caught people's attention, including mine. He was perfectly proportioned and sculpted—not too muscled, not too skinny, broad shoulders, thin waist, long limbs with plenty of definition. Even when he was relaxing, his body looked like it was ready for action.

Freddie hardly ever relaxed, however. I'd seen him around at clubs before—we had the same taste in places to play—and he always seemed to be bouncing around from person to person, talking, hugging, or dancing with whoever was around and willing. And people were always willing to spend time with Freddie, especially girls. He was so open and friendly, it was hard not to like him, even if you knew you shouldn't trust him.

I knew Freddie's reputation. Practically everyone did. He was wild, carefree, and always surrounded by pussy. He was a playboy who loved that title so much and embodied the concept so completely that most people at the clubs actually knew him only as Playboy. It was his nickname, one that I'm almost sure he came up with himself. Still, people used it. And I'm attracted to bad boys. Always have been and still am. Their energy, their charm, their ability to take control of situations. I get bored too easily with nice guys. (I once dated this guy who never took charge of anything. He was always saying to me: Where do *you* want to go? What do *you* want to eat? I'll do whatever *you* want to do. I make a million decisions a day; I can't stand someone who can't make any. It drove me crazy.) Well, Freddie was anything but nice.

I kept an eye on Freddie that night and was dancing near where he was sitting when the Special K wore off and he got his mind back. As soon as he saw me looking at him, he came over and asked me my name. Then, without even a pause, he started trying to convince me to go home with him, "for a night of fun," he said. He didn't waste any time getting to the point, but he did take his time arguing that point, even after I laughed off his invitation. I liked that about him.

After that we danced, we talked, we flirted. Finally Freddie whispered in my ear, "It will be something incredible. You won't regret it."

He was so confident, how could I resist? I let him take me by the hand and lead me through the club toward the door. I walked quickly and tried to cover my face with my hair so no one would see what I was doing. Freddie had a reputation, but so did I. I went to that club a lot, and people knew me as someone you don't fuck around with. I had chosen to leave with Freddie, but I didn't want anyone thinking I was dumb enough to actually fall for his playboy lines. He hadn't fooled me. He just interested me.

In the cab heading across town to his apartment, I was quietly thinking about how I really wanted to handle this situation. I decided that this was going to be just a one-night stand, which meant I needed to stay cold and make sure he knew what I was thinking. When we got to his place, I would tell him up-front that I'd be leaving as soon as I was done. I'd make it clear that *I* was using *him,* and not the other way around. I still hadn't had a real one-night stand since I tried it with Philippe in Montreal and ended up accidentally falling in love. I thought it was past time to try again, but I also wanted him to know what the deal was.

Freddie didn't seem to mind that I wasn't saying much. He just chatted away as he held my hand all the way to his apartment, and continued chatting as he dropped it so he could fish his keys out of his pocket and unlock his front door, still chatting as he grabbed my hand again and led me inside. Nervous as hell, I entered his bedroom. The first thing I saw was a furry creature in the corner looking back at us. It was a cute white rabbit with soft gray wisps. I did a double take, checking to see if it was really alive while Freddie went over and picked it up. It just seemed out of character for this guy to have a pet like that and, even more so, to have one he adored as much as he obviously did. He nuzzled it with his chin, and we sat down on the floor together so Freddie could introduce me to his bunny.

Listening to Freddie talk about his pet got my mind off my anxiety and made me completely forget what I had meant to say to him. It had been a really long week, and I had gone out that night looking for a distraction. I was so tired that I guess I just didn't want to worry about anything for a while. Despite myself, I began to relax. Freddie seemed to sense this and got up to turn on some music—some sassy house beats, just what I liked. It was then that

I gave in to whatever was about to happen. Freddie came back over to me and began to rip my clothes off. Right to the point again. Until we discovered that neither of us had a condom.

We stopped and I called my assistant.

"Can you bring me some condoms?" I asked him, trying not to laugh. I knew the request would embarrass him but he'd still do it. He always did what I asked. "And pick up Justine at the club on your way," I told him. "I don't want her to have to wait for me all by herself. She might as well go home with you."

Justine had flown in from Florida to work for me that week, and we had taken a car together into the city from New Jersey so that we could both have some fun. We felt like we'd earned it. Justine and I have known each other for years, since long before I started my current agency—which is why she is the exception to my rule about not socializing with my girls. I didn't want to leave her stranded at the club, and I had walked out without even telling her where I was going.

When my assistant showed up with my delivery, Justine came with him. That was not part of my plan, and Freddie immediately got the wrong idea. He was all over Justine, and, to my surprise, she was all over him too. Justine should have left with my assistant, who got out of there as quickly as he could, but she didn't. She stayed even though she knew how I felt about sharing men. At that moment, she didn't seem to care. I sat in shock watching as Freddie fucked her. I hadn't even fucked him yet. Finally, I realized that I should put my clothes back on.

As I tried to get my clothes, some of which were still on the bed they were using, Freddie began grabbing at me. He tried to pull me into bed with them. "I do not recycle," I said pointedly, but they just kept on going. At that point I really wasn't feeling very well. The last thing I remember thinking was that I should have left with my assistant. Stunned and dizzy after having been up two days and running, I passed out in the corner of Freddie's bedroom.

When I woke up, I started screaming.

It was the next morning already, and I was mortified that I was still there. Even if things had worked out the way I wanted them to, which obviously they hadn't, I had never meant to stay. It was completely embarrassing.

"I told you I should have gotten us a cab," I heard Justine say from the bed. "I knew she'd be pissed."

I called a car immediately and was out the door with Justine right behind me. All the way home I gave her an earful. I couldn't believe her behavior. She knew better than that. She apologized and told me it was Freddie who wanted me to stay the night undisturbed. (As if that was all that I was upset about.) "He was worried about how tired and stressed out you looked," she told me. How considerate of the asshole who just fucked my so-called friend.

At six o'clock the following morning I got a voice-mail message: "Hi. It's Freddie. Just wondering how you're doing." That was it. No apology. No explanation. Not even a hint of sheepishness in his voice. Just like we'd been friends forever and that night had never happened.

I can't quite explain how the two of us ended up together after that. It doesn't make much sense, given the way things began. But then, love and attraction never have made much sense to me. I can tell you, however, that he was persistent, even pushy, in pursuing me after that, and I like that quality in a man. Less than two weeks later I had checked out of the hotel in New Jersey where I'd been living and moved into his apartment in Manhattan.

It was a power struggle between the two of us from the very beginning. Freddie was used to having women wrapped around his little finger. He just had a way about him that made the ladies fall in line, and he had come to expect it to be that way all the time. But I wasn't used to being controlled by anyone. Not anymore. At first he must have liked the challenge. I liked the challenge too, and on top of that, I got to have the ultimate playboy—the guy every woman wanted—fall in love with me. How could I not love that?

We made big plans together. The first thing we wanted to do was open up a private gambling club in his apartment. We both liked to play and would spend nights at the underground places in Chinatown losing, then winning back, then losing our money again (mostly my money, actually). I figured that, as long as we spent as much money as we did gambling, and as long as so many people we knew did too, some of that money might as well be going into our pockets instead of the pockets of strangers.

I planned to continue with my agency in New Jersey, of course, running it from his apartment. And then maybe, if things went well, eventually he'd help me expand my business into New York. Freddie was such a figure on the club scene that he definitely had the contacts to begin generating a new client list. He really got into the idea, and we talked about what kind of identity we'd create for our new agency to distinguish it from the thousands of others that already existed in the city. We were going to base the concept on Freddie's club personality: "Play like a Playboy!" What man wouldn't want to be Hugh Hefner for a night?

Freddie loved the idea of starting our own empire together, but ultimately, falling in love with a strong woman was too much for his ego to handle. He was jealous of my time and called my work "the other man" in our relationship. He hated being ignored while I pulled all-nighters to get ready for a tour or being asked to hold on while I answered call after call after call on a busy Monday morning. But at the same time, he liked the money I brought in. And he liked the way we sounded together—the Playboy and the Madam. It was as perfect a combination as the Quarterback and the Homecoming Queen.

He felt even more neglected when my friend Mandy called out of the blue to tell me she was coming to New York on a tour with a couple of other girls and she wanted to see me. We hadn't seen each other for two years at that point, not since she had come with me to New Jersey to help me decide if I should start up my business. I was beyond excited that she was coming. Even when we were far away from each other, I still felt like Mandy kept a place in my heart that very few people have ever reached. I considered her a true friend in every possible way.

We decided to meet for lunch the day she arrived, and even though I don't usually have time to socialize during the day, I threw all my work aside so that I could give her my full attention. Freddie, of course, noticed this right away. "Just a few days ago you wouldn't leave your desk for anything, not even to sleep," he complained, "but *now* you can find the time for something besides work?" I tried to explain that this was different because of how much Mandy meant to me and because of how long—too long—it had been since we'd seen each other. No matter what I said, I couldn't make him understand.

I just ignored him after that and did what I wanted to do. It was a good thing too, because it turned out that Mandy was in bad shape. She told me over lunch that her boyfriend, the crazy guy she was always fighting with but really loved and had stuck it out with for years, had just run out on her. He hadn't said good-bye either, just left behind a Dear Jane letter. She hadn't been able to get in touch with him since he left, not even to ask him why. And she hadn't seen it coming at all.

She told me she was fine, just sad, but I could tell that that wasn't true. Her anger showed through her cool jokes until it finally hit her as we were talking. "I've lost the one thing in my whole life that made me happy," she said. After that she just got more and more upset.

I didn't want to leave her alone, so I offered to stay with her in her hotel. Of course, when I told Freddie that, he thought only of himself and got even more pissed off, but I didn't care. I had a real scare the next day, when I left Mandy for a while to get a few things done. After I was finished, I tried calling her so I could meet her back at the hotel, but I couldn't get ahold of her. I called and called, but she didn't answer the phone. I left messages, but she didn't call me back. I was going crazy with worry about what she might have done to herself while I had left her alone.

Finally she did answer her phone. She hadn't done anything to herself, but she had been thinking about it. I rushed right over, feeling guilty and hopeless. Mandy had been there for me before when I had been in a very dark place, and I wanted to help her, but I wasn't sure that I could. How was I going to make her want to live when sometimes I don't even want to live myself? I know it's a horrible thing to think, but sometimes I believe we'd all be better off dead. It's an ugly world, and happiness seems to be this thing that everyone wants and fights one another for, as if there is only a limited amount out there, not enough to go around. But no one ever seems to get to be happy for very long. Who knows what the answer is? I just knew that I desperately wanted my friend to be okay.

Mandy and I locked ourselves in her hotel room for the next few days and talked about everything, *everything,* that was going on in our lives. We even managed to have some fun. And, as tends to happen when I'm with Mandy, she probably ended up helping me more than I helped her. We talked about Freddie, and she got me to see my relationship for what it was—something that wasn't so great. By the time Mandy went back home, I think she was okay and I was really glad that she came.

Talking with Mandy reminded me of something I already believed about relationships: There has to be balance. For example, it would be really hard, if not impossible, for me to have a serious relationship with anyone who didn't have a past of his own. As soon as things went bad between us, any guy could use what I do for a living against me if there wasn't something in his own life that I could use against him too. I also believe that the only way relationships can work is when you don't need each other's money. But that's not how it was with Freddie and me. He was always borrowing money for something, even to take me out. It's not that I cared about the cash. I had money to spare, and I like to share what I have with the people I care about. That's why he was jealous of my work and my friends. He was insecure because I didn't need him, but if he was going to keep up with the lifestyle he'd gotten used to since we'd been together, he did need me. That wasn't good for either of us. If there isn't a balance between what people bring to the table, eventually money always gets in the way.

That's the one and only thing I've figured out about love after all the times I've tried it. Other than that love is something that's still a confusing part of my life. I've yet to conquer it, mentally or emotionally, and usually I think it's best just to stay away from love altogether. After all, emotion is weakness. It was my first love, Andre, who taught me that.

My habit now is to keep a few guys going at the same time so that I never get bored and I never get too serious. (And that doesn't mean sex with all of them, by the way.) That's how I always have someone to keep my mind off the others and off my work when I need a distraction. But sometimes I forget my own rules or choose to ignore them. Freddie was one of those times, and a hard reminder that my rules about love are there for good reason.

The last time I talked to Freddie we were screaming at each other on our cell phones. We'd been fighting for the past several days, and at that moment I couldn't remember if I liked this guy or hated him. In the back of my mind was the question Was I going to take this abuse or do as Andre taught me to do: fuck emotions—maintain my pride and respect at all costs?

Then Freddie said the absolute wrong thing: "You are nothing. You have no friends. You're just a cheap whore from New Jersey, that's all you are."

I knew he was at work when he said it. He was bartending at a friend's restaurant, and I knew he was probably saying these things in front of people. People I knew. Then he told me I had to get the hell out of his apartment right away. We'd been living together for less than a month at that point, but I wasn't going to argue with him anymore. I knew things were over. I told him I'd be right over to pick up my stuff.

"If you go there, I'll have you arrested," he answered, still screaming. "My brother's at my place and he's a cop. He has your hard drive with all your business info on it. You can go to jail for a long time for what you do."

I was stunned. Who was this guy? I obviously didn't know him at all. He definitely didn't know me at all if he was threatening me like that. Playing with my heart is one thing, fucking with my money, my livelihood, my security, my freedom . . . that cannot happen.

On top of everything else, Freddie still had my dog. Max is my heart and a reminder of my time with Mark, who was a much better man. Max had moved into Freddie's place with me, and Freddie loved him right away. He used to take that dog with him everywhere (probably because the dog is a chick magnet), and he, Max, and the bunny would all play together like kids when I was too busy to pay attention to any of them. Now Freddie was threatening to let the dog out into the street.

I hung up the phone and started to think. It was Thursday. On Thursday nights he always went to the bar-lounge Naked Lunch after work . . . The wheels were turning.

I knew someone who could get me a gun quickly, so I called him up to see what he had handy for my protection. He told me he had a .22 that was clean as a whistle and available immediately for $500. I sent my assistant with the cash to pick it up.

Next I called my Asian Boys. I wanted to show Freddie that I did have friends, plenty of them, and they would do just about anything for me. I had known these guys for a while, mostly because I liked to gamble in Chinatown, and they always ran in packs. Very few of them are dangerous alone, but in numbers, it's a different story. I knew I could count on them. They told me they could gather together ten boys to accompany me to the club and fifty more would be nearby. The extras would be available with one phone call if we ran into trouble. I was definitely going to make an impression.

Just over an hour after hanging up on Freddie, I walked into Naked Lunch, .22 loaded, ten gangsters behind me. I ordered a bottle of Hennessy for the boys and a bottle of Veuve Clicquot La Grand Dame Rosé for myself.

Freddie wasn't around. To pass the time, I danced, drank my champagne straight from the bottle, and waited. Soon I spotted some of Freddie's friends—one of his best friends, Nick the Bassist; a photographer whose name I couldn't remember; and some others I'd met when Freddie took me to the Hamptons for Memorial Day weekend. I walked up to them and told them I was celebrating the fact that I was single. The photographer told me that he had broken up with his girlfriend too. He suggested we celebrate together. I ignored him and turned to Nick.

"It's too bad we never finished what we started," I told him.

The party in the Hamptons where I'd met Nick had turned out to be a sex party, something that Freddie had not warned me about when he invited me to the beach for a long weekend. I guess he assumed that, because of what I do, I'd be fine with that sort of thing. But I wasn't. One night, when Freddie was off somewhere else doing god knows what with god knows who, I decided I should get to know his friend Nick the Bassist a little better. I wanted to see if Freddie was as open about relationships as he claimed to be. If he expected me to be fine with him going after any and every girl who walked by, then he wouldn't mind if I took up with just this one boy. The bait worked. Freddie caught us making out and immediately got jealous. He promised he would behave from then on. I thought it was kind of too bad at the time because Nick, I had found out, was a really cool guy. Even though we didn't get around to doing anything serious, Freddie had been mad about it ever since. He couldn't get over the idea that I could be with another man. But, of course, he never had a problem accepting his own double standards.

As I continued to put on my carefree show for Freddie's friends, Nick just stared at me. He leaned in toward me and said, "It's never too late, you know. You tell me when."

"I'll meet you outside in fifteen minutes," I said and danced away.

I went back to my boys to thank them for coming with me. I told them to stay and have a good time but I had changed my mind. We weren't going after Freddie, not tonight. I had other ideas.

Outside, while I waited for Nick, I ran into Jaime the Gambler, another one of Freddie's many friends.

"Freddie's really upset," he said, actually seeming concerned. "He thinks he fucked up."

"He did," I answered.

"He was just upset. He didn't know what he was saying. You should give him twenty-four hours to calm down and then you two can talk this out."

"I should give *him* time to calm down? He won't let me go home. He's holding all my stuff hostage. I don't even have any clean clothes. And he threatened me. And my dog! He totally crossed the line."

Jaime looked like he was about to protest, but I was done talking to him. And then, perfect timing, there was Nick. I was glad Jaime saw us leave together, because I knew that word would get around. I hated Freddie and I wanted him to know it.

First Nick and I tried to go to a hotel around the corner, but it was all booked up. Then he suggested we go to Seb's house, which was perfect. It was Seb's house in the Hamptons where things had started to go wrong between Freddie and me, so it might as well be Seb's house in the city where they ended for good.

I've always believed that to truly get over someone you have to replace him. And once you fuck someone else, there's no turning back. It's the best way for me to end a relationship and force my emotions not to take over. That night I fucked the shit out of Nick, right in front of Seb and his girlfriend in fact. That night I had my first one-night stand . . . finally.

Later I went to Freddie's apartment by myself. I still had my keys, and by that time I had calmed down enough to realize he had probably been bluffing about getting his brother to arrest me. Freddie had too many reasons of his own not to want the police in his apartment. As soon as I walked in, Max came bounding over to greet me. The rest of my stuff was in another room, behind a locked door that I didn't have a key for. I banged on it and screamed. There was no sound but I know that Freddie probably was there. He had once told me that he lost the key to that door and without it there was no way to lock it from the outside.

I still had my gun with me, and for a moment I thought about shooting down the door. But I quickly realized it wasn't worth it. If I was going to go to jail for having an unregistered gun, I at least wanted the satisfaction of shooting the man himself, not just his door. Max was running wild around my feet. He was overdue for a walk anyway. I picked him up and we left.

Max and I got a car back to New Jersey and checked into another hotel. The next day I sent my assistant to pick up my things. Freddie didn't give him any trouble. I think he had made his point and I had made mine. There was nothing left to fight about.

I've come to realize that I'm just unlucky in love. But I've also been around long enough and had enough experience to know that things like this don't happen to me by complete accident. As

I've said before, I believe in karma, so I know a lot of it is my own fault. I've screwed over too many guys in my past, and those kinds of things come back around to haunt a person. That's why I make a point of treating people fairly in my work . . . the girls who work for me, my customers. I treat those people the same way I want them to treat me, and that usually works out fine for all of us. But love is another matter.

I've spent most of my life searching for someone to care about me, no matter who it is. Sometimes it hits me that I have no value in this world and that, if I should die, there is a good chance it wouldn't affect anyone and it would go unnoticed by everyone except my clients. For a while I could pretend that Freddie might be the one who cared if something bad happened to me. After him, there was Justin, a guy I lived with on the Jersey Shore until he started doing drugs and lying to his credit card company about which one of us owed them money. Both of them actually had me convinced for a while that they truly cared about me.

There are only four things that I'm deathly afraid of: commitment, heights, Vegas, and Elvis. The first two are pretty obvious, I think. Vegas is because it's a gambling Mecca and just the kind of place where I know I would really lose my head and maybe never get it back. I don't know why Elvis really; I just think he's creepy. And maybe because there are lots of them in Vegas. Every time I see an Elvis impersonator I think, What if that's the real Elvis back from the dead and no one knows it because there are so many goddamn Elvis impersonators out there that we can't tell the difference anymore? I wonder, if that happened, would it make the real Elvis happy that he could finally live his life in peace, or sad that his true identity was going unnoticed? I can't decide which would be better for someone like him, and the whole thing just messes with my head.

Not long ago, when I was with Justin, I came up with a plan to face my fears. One night, soon after we got together, when we were still really into each other, we started talking about getting married. I decided then that the best, most romantic thing I could ever do with anyone would be to hop a plane for Las Vegas, get one of those Elvis impersonator–ministers to marry us, and then jump out of a plane to seal the deal. That way I could face all of my fears at once, in a single day, and put them all behind me.

I still think it's a good idea. We never did it, of course, but we talked about it, and he was game for a while. If there is ever a way you could reset your karma, kind of start over with a clean slate, I think it would be by doing something like that. Maybe I just need one really big moment when I could face all my demons at once.

CHAPTER 12

Functional Family

Lately, despite my rules, I've been more open to letting people into my life. I don't think I'll ever get married or settle down with a guy, for all the obvious reasons. Even if I found someone who didn't turn out to be an asshole, I probably still wouldn't trust the relationship. Between my own parents; my clients, who are mostly married; and the relationships I've seen my girls and girlfriends go through, I'm not sure I believe in the whole "until death do us part" thing.

But I'm beginning to form my own attachments. First off there's my dog, Max, who has remained my companion through some hard times and several relationships. He's the man in my life these days, the best one I've ever had.

And more recently there's been Zoe, who I met when I was in Montreal. She was about eighteen then and already working the trade, which is what she's done for a living ever since. Like I said before, I like to bring in girls from Montreal from time to time because there is a lot of experienced talent there. As Zoe puts it, practically every halfway-decent-looking girl there tries out the sex trade at one time or another. She may be exaggerating a bit but probably not much. I brought Zoe to New Jersey about a year ago for what was supposed to be just a week of work. She ended up deciding to stay here permanently. She wanted to get away from her pimp, who had controlled her life for a long time. Leaving the country seemed like the best way to do that.

Zoe is a soft-spoken blonde with a slight French accent, and she is definitely the sex kitten type. She's got long, thick hair, the body of a pinup girl, and perfect fake tits—big, but not frighteningly big like Pamela Anderson's, and still pretty soft and natural to the touch (at least that's what the guys tell me). She's been working for a number of years now, and she's great at her job. The clients love her, so I had no reason to discourage her from sticking around. But our relationship became much more than just madam and call girl.

At the time that Zoe moved here, I was looking to expand my business. It had been running pretty consistently for several years, and I wanted to see where I could take it next. I could only do so much by myself, however, and I had dreams of expanding into other areas of New Jersey and even into other cities, like Boston and Philadelphia. Even if I worked night and day, I wouldn't be able to pull all that off on my own, so I worked out a deal with Zoe to become my support staff.

Zoe has a nice voice, and I have spent way too much of my life on the phone, which is actually the part of the job that drives me crazy. The arrangement was this: when Zoe wasn't with clients, she'd work the phones and book and confirm appointments. She'd also occasionally handle e-mail requests for appointments, though I still like to do most of the computer work myself. In exchange I gave her a place to live. I had a big two-bedroom apartment at the time and wasn't using the other room, so she moved in. After that we became more than business associates. We became room-mates and friends.

I still do all the marketing and business strategy—I'm not sure there's anyone I'd ever trust to do that for me—but in terms of client relations, Zoe is great. She never gets annoyed and never gets angry. She's a bit passive, and sometimes she doesn't know how to handle a situation, like when a client complains about a girl being late for an appointment, but when that happens she just puts the guy on hold and asks me what to do. In extreme situations, she simply hands the phone over to me. I'm usually not far away.

When issues do arise, how I choose to handle the situation has to do with who I'm talking to. I've gotten to know my customers really well over the years. Girls are often late for appointments because I like to book them pretty close together when I can so that we don't waste any time. If the previous guy was late or the girl needs a break for one reason or another—she needs some food to refuel, or a chance to freshen up, or whatever—that can mean a client has to wait downstairs or in the parking lot for ten, fifteen, sometimes thirty minutes, which can make the poor guy very unhappy. Sometimes it's enough just to assure the guy that his hour won't start until he gets into the room and that I'll even tack some extra time on the end to thank him for waiting. That's for the type of guy who is concerned about getting his money's worth. (They almost never use the extra time anyway because very few guys need the whole hour to get done what they need to get done.) Other guys get annoyed with waiting because they're worried it will kill their mood. To guys like that I say, in my sweetest tone, something like "I'm so sorry about the delay, sweetie. I'll let you smack her ass to make up for it." That usually does it. But that's exactly the kind of work I'm getting fed up with doing. And Zoe's getting better at it.

Zoe's a very friendly, very outgoing person, and having her around has changed things for me. I've always gone out lots, but now I stay in more and have people over. That's a big step for me.

I also think I'm more open with people, some people anyway. If I hadn't been that way, I probably barely would have noticed Melissa when she came over. She was a mousy thing when I first met her—tall, nearly five ten, with short, dark hair, and kind of goofy. She wasn't quiet exactly, just timid and a bit naïve, the kind of girl you know you can easily convince to do anything you want her to. I like powerful people, which she definitely wasn't, so she just wasn't the type of girl who usually makes an impression on me.

The first time I met Melissa it was through my friend Lucas. Lucas was a serious tweaker, into any kind of club drug he could get his hands on, and I'd run into him when I was out on the town all the time. He was funny and strange, and I liked him but I never really trusted him beyond being someone to party with.

One day he called me up and told me he had this girlfriend who was in the business and asked if I needed any new employees. I'm always looking for new talent and I take referrals, so I asked him what she looked like and where she'd worked before. I don't remember what he said exactly, just that his description of her sounded pretty good. Lucas is a slick guy, and I didn't suspect anything, not yet.

Lucas also explained that the places Melissa had worked before had been pretty low-tech, so she didn't have any pictures or reviews on any of the sites. That happens sometimes, so I wasn't too concerned about it because I know how to deal with that type of situation. I just figured she'd been a low-class hooker up until then and she was looking to upgrade. I told him we could build her online presence and work with her to get some good reviews to establish a reputation with the right kinds of clients. I also told him that it wouldn't be easy and that she'd have to work with me to make it happen, but it was definitely doable. He said she was all for it and would do whatever I thought was necessary.

The first step was to get some pictures of her to post on our site. Unless the client knows me well enough to trust my judgment and description—and I do have a few of those—he almost always wants to look at a picture before scheduling an appointment. Occasionally a client will call up a little desperate and ask who I've got available right away, what she looks like, and then he'll just take what he can get, but usually my clients prefer to wait for the girl they want, as long as they don't have to wait too long.

We can't use just any old photos either. We're not making a MySpace page. This is a business. The photos need to be sexy, they need to be full body, and most important, they need to be accurate. Even though a girl gets dressed up and primped for her photos, they need to represent what she really looks like. More than once I've had a client show up for an appointment and then turn around and leave as soon as the girl opened the door. Maybe she's gained weight or is older than she looked in her pics or just hasn't been taking care of herself or is having a bad day, but clients can be picky about those kinds of things. Seeing a girl's photo is the start of a fantasy, and if the girl spoils that fantasy right up-front, well then, why would a guy pay for that? It's much better to get pictures taken regularly that show what a girl really looks like rather than posting some outdated or airbrushed thing that she'll never live up to. That way, a client knows what he's in for and I get fewer phone calls asking to reschedule with someone else.

Because photos are so important in this business and there really is an art to them, I wanted to talk to Melissa before she had a photo shoot. I knew she was new to this kind of thing, so I made my rules perfectly clear. I have a couple of photographers I work with regularly, and they are professionals who know exactly what I want, but they come at a price. Since the girls in this business are usually not too good with money, I've worked out two payment options: (1) The entertainer can cover the costs of the photos, which means she owns them outright and grants us the right to use them only on our site to advertise her services and they will be taken down, upon her request, within three to five business days; or (2) We can share the cost of the photos, in which case the company owns the copyright to them and can do with them what we wish until we have been reimbursed in full. After that, the copyright reverts to the entertainer, who can then use the photos for other jobs or other agencies or can just ask us not to use them. Melissa didn't have any money, so she took the second option. She didn't ask too many questions, but she agreed to my terms. I also got the feeling she had no idea how to take a good picture, so I decided I'd better be there for the shoot. We made an appointment for her to come to my place for a session with one of my photographers.

When Melissa arrived, she made a good first impression. She was more cute than sexy, but I immediately saw how I could give her a coed persona and sell her that way. I was a little surprised that she didn't bring much with her, but I always have lots of lingerie and makeup around, so I knew I could find something for her to wear. I started talking to my photographer about what I wanted, and Zoe, who was back from a call, started talking to Melissa. Zoe can talk to practically anyone about nothing at all.

I could see out of the corner of my eye that Melissa liked the attention Zoe was paying her, so I let them keep chatting for a while. Melissa was a bit shy, and Zoe seemed to be getting her to come out of her shell, which I needed her to do if these pictures were going to be any good. In the meantime, the photographer and I were going through some clothes and backdrops to set up the right look.

My ears perked up when I heard Zoe ask, "How old are you anyway?"

"Uh, twenty-two," Melissa answered.

"Really?" Zoe said. "You're almost my age! I thought you were younger."

Zoe went on to another subject, but for some reason an alarm went off in my head. I asked Zoe if I could talk to her in the other room for a minute about some business stuff. The shoot was being set up in the living room of our apartment, so we went into my bedroom and I whispered, "How old do you think she really is?"

"I don't know," Zoe said, immediately getting the hint, "but I think she's young. You can just tell by talking to her."

"Let's both ask her again," I said, and we went back into the living room and sat down next to Melissa on the couch.

"How old are you?" I asked her straight out, while trying not to sound like I was accusing her of anything.

"Uh . . . like, twenty-two," she said. She sounded a bit scared.

"No, you can't be that old," Zoe said. "When were you born?"

She didn't know the answer to that, and pretty soon we wore her down. "I'm seventeen," she finally admitted. She was giggling when she said it, like she'd been a bad girl, but it wasn't funny to me.

"You should not be doing this," I told her. "At your age, you should be in school. What are you doing here? Why did Lucas tell me you were older?"

At that, Melissa broke down. Her façade was pretty flimsy anyway, and it melted right away as soon as I hit the right button. Lucas was the right—or should I say the wrong—button. Melissa got really upset, and when she finally started talking, her story just spilled out.

"Lucas has been making me do this," she said. "It started just a few days after I moved in with him. He was the one who asked *me* to live with him, and he'd been great up until then, so I thought it would be great. But then all of a sudden, everything was about money. I had to pay my share of the rent, he said, and the groceries and the expenses, even the drugs, which he'd given me for free until then. I told him I'd find a job, but he said that would take too long and whatever job I could find wouldn't be enough anyway. He said he knew something I could do to make money.

"When I got home one day after that, there was this car waiting to take me to an appointment. Lucas had set it up. I didn't know what to do, so I got in the car. Everything had been awful for me for months anyway, so I barely cared what was happening. I hardly even remember what the guy looked like. When I got home, Lucas took all my money. 'You only have to do it for three weeks,' he told me, 'until we have enough money to get by.' But that didn't happen. He called you because he knows you'll be able to get me more clients and that you charge them more. That's all he cares about, the money."

It turned out Melissa was a runaway. She'd had some problems with her family and with the law, so she had ended up in a juvenile facility in upstate New York. Remind you of anyone? I could definitely relate. It was an awful place, so she escaped as often as she could. Usually they'd find her pretty quickly and haul her back, but one time, thanks to some Hare Krishna guy who gave her money for bus fare, she made it all the way to New York City with nothing but the clothes on her back. "Be good, God is watching," the Krishna had told her when he gave her the cash. She thought it was hysterical that the guy had said that to her.

She had nowhere to go, so she'd been sleeping on the E train when she met Lucas and his friend Tim, and they lured her to New Jersey with the promise of drugs and a safe place to hang out. She was into coke at the time, but they introduced her to meth. It was fun in the beginning, and things started off slowly. She'd come and go, sometimes sleeping on Lucas's couch when he let her; it was as safe and secure a place as she'd been in months. Finally one night he said to her, "You're going to be my girlfriend." He should have said, "You're going to be my meal ticket." But she didn't know any better. She liked him, so she agreed.

I decided right then and there that Melissa was not going back to Lucas's place—no way. She would stay with us. Zoe not only agreed, she was excited. I think she thought she'd finally have a playmate. That's how Zoe, Melissa, and I became a family, our own screwed-up version of a Norman Rockwell picture.

The next day we all went to Lucas's apartment together to pick up Melissa's things. We intentionally hadn't called him to let him know that his "girlfriend" wouldn't be coming home . . . ever. I thought he'd probably throw a fit and destroy all her stuff or try to sell it, the cheap bastard. In case we ran into trouble, I brought Tony, one of my very big Mafia friends, along for the ride. As we drove to Lucas's place, we told him Melissa's story, and he was disgusted by it. Those Mafia boys have a strict moral code, especially when it comes to women and children. He said that if Lucas was there, he'd teach him a lesson for free.

Melissa just acted like she was on some adventure. She looked a lot older than she was, but it was moments like that one when it would really hit me—she was still just a kid. I mean, it was like she was on her way to Disneyland or something.

When we got there, Lucas was home, of course. He didn't work, so he had nowhere to be. Melissa gathered up her clothes while we asked him for the money she'd made. "You told me you were just saving it for me," Melissa screamed at him, "so where is it?" Naturally, it was all gone.

Lucas started cursing at Melissa after that. But before any of us got a chance to respond, Tony hit him, hard, and he fell back against the wall, then down to the floor. It was just one punch, but that's all that was needed. I knew bringing Tony was a good idea.

On the way home Melissa asked Tony why he'd hit Lucas. "He was pissing me off and I didn't like the way he disrespected you," he said. Melissa smiled the biggest smile I'd seen from her so far, and I think she developed a little crush on him right then and there. The rest of the way home Tony lectured her on how she needed to get her act together and get an education. Melissa just listened and agreed.

Because Lucas had basically been running her life, I wanted Melissa to know that she had some say about what happened to her, so I asked her if she wanted to stay with us for a while or go somewhere else. I knew she would say she wanted to stay with us, but I thought it was important to give her the option. She was as happy as a little puppy about the idea.

But then I told her, if she was going to stay with us, there would be some rules she had to follow, no exceptions. First, there would be no more working for her of any kind. And no more drugs either. She and Lucas had been experimenting with all sorts of substance cocktails, but I told her that had to stop. I wasn't going to be a hypocrite, so I told her that I sometimes indulged in such things, as did Zoe, but that was okay for us because we were adults. She was a kid, and she needed to start acting like one.

I also told her, and I knew it would be a sticking point, that we had to call her mom. We didn't need to tell her where she was living exactly, but we did need to let her know that Melissa was okay and give her the cell number where she could reach us.

Melissa's mom was really angry at first when I called, but I just told her that Melissa was welcome to stay with me but I wanted her to know what was going on and that she was okay. As the days and weeks passed, I kept calling just to let Melissa's mom know what her daughter was up to. When we wanted to take a trip to Boston for the weekend one time, I called up Melissa's mom to ask her if it was okay. She seemed stunned by the question. "Yeah, sure, do what you want," she said, but she didn't sound angry this time. I think she actually appreciated the updates.

I know what you're thinking, some family—an illegal immigrant/call girl, an underage felon, and me. We had fun together though. We started calling Melissa Felonie after that, "because she'll get you twenty to life." Zoe and I both treated her like a little sister. Since my apartment was only a two-bedroom and both bedrooms were already taken, we had trouble figuring out where to put her. It was funny because I had lived there by myself for months before Zoe moved in, and it had seemed really big then. Now it felt tight, but no one seemed to mind and we worked it out. Sometimes Melissa slept on the big couch in the living room, sometimes in bed with one or the other of us like we were having a slumber party.

Because Melissa wasn't going to school and I wouldn't let her work—not even answer the phones—she sometimes got bored and in the way. I tried to make up assignments for her to keep her busy, as if she were in school. She liked to draw and was really good at it, so I told her to draw pictures of the people she'd met. She also said she was interested in writing, so I told her to write about what had happened to her. She'd take Max for walks and hang out with Zoe when she wasn't working, but Melissa had a lot of energy and an active mind, and I could tell that life with us wasn't going to be enough for her forever.

Fortunately, about that time Nicole became an honorary member of our odd little family. Nicole had worked on and off for me for months. She's in her forties, divorced, and has two kids, but she's the cutest little blonde you've ever seen. She also has a phenomenal body. No one would ever guess how old she is, and those clients who know couldn't care less.

During the week, Nicole's kids live with their dad, who also supports Nicole and paid for the house she lives in in New Jersey. It was all part of the divorce settlement. Nicole's ex is a trip. He once told her that if he could have had kids by himself and left the woman (meaning her) out of it, he would have, but thanks to his biological limitations, he had to put up with her and pay up as well. But Nicole was well taken care of. She just worked for me so she'd have some pocket money to pay for her G (short for GHB) habit.

Because Nicole didn't need to work, she was often home during the day without much to do. I began shipping Melissa off to her house when she was getting on my nerves or when I was really busy. It turned out to be a perfect solution for everyone because they ended up really liking each other.

I was the one who always called Melissa's mom, but after a while they finally agreed to speak to each other directly. When Melissa got on the phone with her mother for the first time, they talked for a long while. By the end they had decided that her mom should come down for a visit. We arranged to meet her one weekend at Nicole's house. I thought it would be better if she didn't see our place. There might be too much incriminating evidence around, and besides, I didn't want her to be able to track me down if she ever found out the whole story about what I did for a living and what had happened to her daughter.

Her mom showed up one Saturday with Melissa's brother and stepdad. We were all there to support Melissa—me, Zoe, Nicole, and even Nicole's kids, who were with her for the weekend. We tried our best to come across as normal, well-adjusted people, but everyone seemed a little nervous, especially Melissa. She wasn't sure what to say to her mom about what she'd been doing all this time.

"The truth doesn't always set you free," I advised her. "It can also lock you up."

In this case, it could have locked me up too, so I didn't want to get into it. But I did want her mom to know something about what Melissa had been through so she would understand how dangerous it had been for her daughter when she was on her own. She easily could have ended up a junkie ho like Natasha, or the property of some pimp like Zoe had been for years, or worse. And you can't just come back from things like that. I know. I've seen it happen way too many times. I wanted her mom to have some clue about what can happen to a young girl if she's left on her own with no one looking out for her, so I told her, without mentioning my part in it, of course, that Lucas had tried to pimp Melissa. Her mom just gasped and looked at me. I think she was deciding whether to believe me or not. Melissa was a big drama queen, always overstating things or just plain making them up to get attention, so I got the feeling her mom had decided a long time ago not to believe much of what her daughter said. But this wasn't coming from Melissa, it was coming from me, and I'd always been straight with her when we talked on the phone. I may have left out some details, but I never lied to her.

When Melissa's mom saw us all acting like one big happy family, with Nicole and her kids and Zoe and me all laughing and having fun, I think she felt guilty. I think she saw that Melissa was capable of being part of a family and that maybe some of what had happened between them had been her fault too. After all, she's the adult. Melissa is just starting to figure things out, and she clearly has a long way to go.

Melissa went home with her parents that day, and I haven't seen her since. She keeps in touch though. Last time I talked to her she had gotten some little ten-dollar-an-hour job, but she thought it was okay. And she was working on getting her GED so she could go to college. She wanted to go to art school, which seemed like a good idea because she was so into drawing, and she was going to visit her dad for the first time in a while. She sounded good. A bit unsure of herself but excited about things and not so angry or scared anymore. I think that's what a girl her age should sound like, but what do I know about things like that? When I was her age, I was running a brothel in New York and living with some drug dealer twenty years older than me, a guy who cheated on me constantly and, when he'd done too much smack, would knock me around. That was who was looking out for me when I was her age.

I hope things work out for Melissa, but who knows? This world can be tough on young girls, and the ones who have done what she's done tend to fall back on it when times get rough and they're having problems paying the rent. "Once a ho always a ho," as people in my world like to say. Maybe Melissa will change her life, but I can't pretend I don't know the odds, and they are long. Still, a girl her age deserves a second chance, doesn't she?

CHAPTER 13

A Sunday in the Life
of a Very Young Madam

Even I need a day of rest, so on Sundays my business is officially closed. (Our hours, as advertised, are Monday through Friday, 9:00 A.M. to 11:00 P.M.) My assistants are off. I keep one available to me on Saturdays for errands and other work matters, like taking girls to the airport so they can fly home after working for the week. But on Sundays both of my assistants are free to ignore me, even if I do sometimes find reasons to call them.

Even though Sunday could be a great time to make lots of money, I have designated it as my quiet day, because it's a day that my friends or boyfriends usually have off too, and because I tend to go out on Friday and Saturday nights, which means I need Sundays to recover. Sunday is, however, a popular day for clients. Over the years I've learned a few things about the male mind-set, and one thing I can tell you is that, in a lot of ways, they all think alike, especially when it comes to sex.

For instance, you'd think Friday would be a popular night in my line of work. The workweek is over and it's time to let off steam. Paychecks usually come down on Fridays, so guys feel like they have money in their pockets. But while my phone certainly does ring on Friday afternoons, Fridays are nothing like Monday mornings, when it's practically off the hook for hours at a time.

Mondays, with the stress of the coming week lying in wait right in front of them—that's when men feel like they need my services the most.

In the minds of most men, Fridays are for their girlfriends, Saturdays are for their wives, and Sundays are for themselves, which means when they aren't out drinking with their buddies or watching football (or after they're done drinking with their buddies and watching football), they often call me, hoping that, even though our offices are closed, I'll make an exception.

Sunday is also a big day for businessmen. My clients are all professional types, so many of them travel regularly for work. They tend to fly in Sunday evening so they can start work bright and early Monday morning. But after they check in to their hotel rooms, what are they supposed to do? They're alone in an unfamiliar city. They're bored. They have nothing to do until tomorrow, and it's still the weekend. That's when they call me.

Customers who are frequent travelers and know all too well what it's like to be bored and alone on a Sunday evening will often ask me in advance to make arrangements for them. They call me at the same time they're choosing their hotel and reserving their rental car. With enough warning, I'm happy to accommodate good customers, even on my day off, which is what happened one particular Sunday night not long ago. One of my very best regulars had told me that he'd be staying in New York for the week and made special arrangements months in advance to meet with a girl after he arrived. He agreed to pay extra for a trip into Manhattan, since I usually work only in New Jersey. He was even willing to be flexible about the time, so I told him I'd figure something out for him. He asked only that the girl be someone new (new to him, that is).

I had booked Danielle weeks ago. She wasn't just new to the client, she was new to me too. She had never worked for me before, but she came highly recommended by another girl who had been with me for a while. It seemed like a good opportunity to try her out. I'd seen her pictures. I'd also read her reviews, and it was clear she knew what she was doing. Unfortunately, I hadn't been able to convince either of my assistants to work the extra day, so I was going to have to chauffeur her myself. The appointment wasn't until around 9:00 P.M., and she could take a car there directly from the airport, but afterward I was going to have to pick her up and take her to her hotel in New Jersey, where she'd be working for the rest of the week. The client had asked for extra time—two hours—so she wouldn't really need me until about 11:00, plenty of time for me to have my leisurely Sunday.

My plan for the day was to do some errands, maybe meet a friend, stock up on groceries at the Korean market for my boyfriend Justin and me, and ignore my phone as much as possible. I'd been off for two whole weeks, and that Sunday was the last day of my vacation. I wanted it to be as low-key as possible.

When I had decided to take the time off, I told everyone—my clients, my girls, and my assistants—that I was eloping. That way they couldn't be too upset that I was shutting down without warning. The problem is, I am my business. If I'm not there to run it, no work will get done.

I didn't really get married. What I was doing was cleaning out my system. I've had ulcers for years from all the stress in my life, and at that point they'd become unbearable. I was taking every painkiller I could get my hands on just to make it through the day—Percocet, Vicodin, even morphine patches I got from a customer who works as a pharmaceutical rep. The rep gave me some samples in exchange for a complimentary appointment with the lady of his choice. I hadn't realized that a lot of those medicines could actually make my ulcers a whole lot worse after a while. Justin finally convinced me I needed to stop taking them all at once in order to let my body recover. That's when I moved into his house on the Jersey Shore. He took care of me, and god, the pain was awful. But no one needed to know what I'd really been doing. All they needed to know was that I would be unavailable until further notice.

That particular Sunday afternoon, I was driving along the highway following the Jersey coastline. I had my sunroof open, a CD of my favorite DJ mixes playing with the volume cranked, and the GPS navigation system on my new BMW talking to me every now and then, telling me in its reassuring lady-computer voice when to turn and where to stop. When my phone, which was resting in my lap, started ringing the first time, I ignored it. But when it rang a second time, I look down and recognized Danielle's number. She was one of the few people I knew I needed to talk to that day.

"Hi, honey. What's up?"

"Hi, it's Danielle. Listen, I'm having problems finding a flight that gets in on time. They're all either booked up or really expensive."

"Where are you, honey?"

"I'm still in Florida."

Typical ho. It was already noon and she was just starting to figure out how she was going to get here in time for her appointment that night. We had agreed when I booked her that she'd arrive in the early evening to give her plenty of time to meet the client. But I wasn't surprised. She was no more or less flaky than any other girl in this business. Occupational hazard.

"Where are you checking, sweetie?"

"Priceline."

"Into which airport?"

"La Guardia."

"Try Newark, honey. You can also try JFK, but try Newark first."

"Where's that?"

"Newark's in New Jersey, sweetie. It's practically right across the river from Manhattan and it's near me. Try all three airports. Are you at your computer now?"

"Yes."

"Well, try that right now, and if you have any problems, call me back. And we want you in as early as possible, sweetie, okay? As *early* as possible."

"Okay."

I like to drive fast, and I realized as I hung up that I had gradually sped up to 110 miles per hour. As I put my phone back in my lap, I started to slow down. I lost my driver's license a while back, so the last thing I needed was to get pulled over. "Exit approaching in twenty seconds . . . ten seconds . . . five seconds . . . turn now," my GPS told me. God, I love that thing.

The Korean market was about forty minutes away from where Justin and I lived, but it was worth the trip. It's huge and has everything, and I planned to stock up for an entire month. Justin had lost some weight recently—I thought then that it was because he'd been working so much, but I would soon find out it was because he was doing lots of drugs behind my back—and I had decided that I needed to fatten him up.

As I loaded my cart to the top with tubs of freshly made kimchi, ribs marinated in the store's special sauce, lots of vegetables, and candies with cartoon figures on the packages, my phone rang again. I put it away in my purse for later. At the bakery counter, I tried a sample of a doughy pancake just fried and spread with a lumpy red bean paste. The taste was familiar and I was sure I'd had this before, when I was living in Korea, but the memory was so distant I couldn't remember where I had been or who I was with.

As I filled the trunk and backseat of my car with grocery bags, I checked my phone to see whose call I had missed. It was a client who was a real regular. Knowing him, he'd probably had a pretty hard time over the past couple weeks, when he couldn't get ahold of me. I knew he had called several times, so as I pulled out of the parking lot, I decided to be nice and call him back.

"Hi there. It's me," I said when he answered the phone. I was sure he knew my voice.

"Hi. I've been trying to reach you," he said.

"I know. I got your messages. Are you looking for something this week?"

"Actually, I was wondering about tonight."

"We don't usually work Sundays, you know that."

"I know, but I have some time to myself tonight, so I was just hoping . . ."

"Well, I do have a girl flying in this evening. I'm not sure when she's arriving, but I can see if she'll have time for you."

"That'd be great. Any time. I'm here watching the game, so whenever. Will you let me know? Or should I check back with you later?"

"I should know more soon. After I get home and have a chance to call her, I'll let you know what her schedule is."

"Great. Thanks. So when do you think that'll be?"

"Oh, probably an hour or so."

"Okay. You know we've missed you lately. How was it? Did you really get married?"

"It was great. Thanks for asking."

"Well . . . congratulations."

"Thanks. I'll call you back as soon as I can, okay, baby?"

"Okay."

The phone calls had put me back into work mode, and since I still had a half-hour drive to get home, I decided to do a little housekeeping. First, I called my friend in the city and left him a message saying I'd be coming in late that night and could drop off the money I owed him if he was around. I always pay my debts right away.

Next, because I was thinking about debts, I called Angelita. She was another new girl who was supposed to work for me a couple of weeks before but never showed up. Angelita was recommended to me by Sherry, another local madam I swapped girls with sometimes. Doing business with Sherry was always a potential problem, because we had very different standards and policies and sometimes the girls got confused. She was much more laid-back, and she'd take just about anyone she could find to work.

Angelita had been given my handbook, however, just like any other girl, so she should have known what I expected. My rules about money are very straightforward. Since girls travel from all over the place to work for me and they always stay in three-star hotels, where their appointments take place, there are obviously certain expenses involved. I'm happy to help make arrangements and get the best prices (something I'm an expert at by this point), but each girl is responsible for paying her share. That means airfare, hotel, car services (though I'm also happy to have my assistants serve as drivers for the week at reasonable rates), and anything else they might need. As for Angelita, I booked a hotel for her for the week, and, according to the handbook, even if she never did a day of work for me, she still owed me for part of that hotel bill.

I had already called Angelita several times since she ditched her obligations, but up until that day I had only gotten her voice mail. This time, however, she picked up the phone, so I got right to the point. I didn't ask her what happened because I didn't care. The last thing I wanted to do was listen to a bunch of excuses or another sob story from another girl. I simply told her what I tell them all in these situations, that we had some settling up to do and that I'd be happy to work it out with her in any number of ways. Since I'd been on vacation, I hadn't had time to line up many girls to work for me for the coming week, and I was worried that as soon as I sent out an e-mail blast to my client list saying I was back, I'd have more clients calling than I could handle. So I also told Angelita that if she wanted to work for me that week, we could take what she owed me out of what she made.

"Okay," she agreed. "But I can't work until Thursday. I'm already working for Sherry Monday through Wednesday."

"Okay, then. I'll book you for Thursday and Friday. I think I'll put you in Princeton or maybe the Meadowlands. How early can you be there on Thursday?"

"I can be in the Meadowlands any time you want. I can even be there Wednesday night late."

"Are you that close by? Where does Sherry have you on Wednesday?"

"I'm working there, in the Meadowlands. Monday through Wednesday."

"The Meadowlands?"

My territory in New Jersey is a very big deal to me, and I'm very protective of it. It's one of the reasons I set up shop in New Jersey instead of New York, because I knew that I had the best access to clients and that no one could match my service. When I came to New Jersey, the market was wide open, and I basically created the upscale market here from scratch.

I had met Sherry at a club in New York. We knew a lot of the same people and had partied together many times. I considered her a casual friend, so when she and her sister had decided to open up their own agency the year before, I was fine with it. She came to me for advice and I gave it to her, but I also said very specifically that I would help her out as long as she stayed out of my territory. She could have South Jersey because I didn't want to be that spread out, but Princeton, Edison, New Brunswick, Newark, *the Meadowlands,* these places belonged to me. And I'd been sending tons of clients her way. Any time one of my guys was heading down to Atlantic City, I hooked him up with her. Not anymore.

"I didn't know that," Angelita said nervously after I explained why I was so upset. "But that's between you guys. I mean, she just told me where to go. I didn't ask to go there. You need to talk to her."

"You understand what I'm saying, though, right?" I said.

"Yeah, I understand, but . . ."

"Here's what I'm going to do. I'm going to book you for the Meadowlands all this week. Do you already have a hotel?"

"Yeah. I'm staying at the Sheraton."

"Okay. When you get there tomorrow, call me. I'm going to put you on my site and send out an e-mail advertising that you'll be there all week. So that way, when Sherry has you just sitting around waiting for your next appointment, I can send you some real work. And I guarantee you'll make more money with me. Way more. Okay?"

"Okay, I guess."

"So you'll call me tomorrow morning?"

"Yeah, okay. But what do I tell Sherry?"

"You don't have to tell her anything. That's between her and me."

"Yeah. It's between the two of you. Okay. I'll call you tomorrow."

The rest of the way home I was pissed. For a minute, I thought I might call Sherry and confront her—I wanted to tell her what I thought of the really stupid thing she'd been doing behind my back—but I knew it was better to just swallow it and not say a thing. I didn't want her to know what I knew. Not yet. When I got home, Justin heard the car pull up and came outside to help me with the groceries.

"You'll never guess what just happened," I said to him.

I told him about Sherry as he looked through the bags to see what I had brought home. "Did you talk to Sherry?" he asked when I'd finished my story.

"No. I don't have to talk to her. She knows better than that. Now not only am I going to take away her girls, starting with Angelita, I'm going to take over her territory—Atlantic City, South Jersey, even Philly, because she goes there sometimes. Remember this morning when I said I wasn't ready to go back to work yet? Well, now I'm motivated. I need to go inside and make a few calls. I've got this girl coming in tonight and another guy I'm juggling who wants to see her now too, and he's willing to wait until whenever, and I need to start booking Angelita for first thing tomorrow because she'll go where the money is. They all go where the money is. Money is the only real loyalty around here. Can you finish taking in the groceries, sweetie?"

"Yeah. I'm hungry. Did you get anything good?"

"Yeah, I got lots of good stuff, but just wait a little bit and I'll make you dinner. I just need a little while to sort some things out first, but I want to make you dinner."

"Okay."

A lot of things changed in my life after that day. That was one of the last good days I remember between Justin and me. It was not long after that that I caught him taking drugs and we broke up. After that day I became super-focused on work for a while too, which is probably why I didn't notice right away that he was acting strangely. He'd been taking pills at the same time that he'd been helping me get off them.

It was also not long after that day that I dismantled my business and went into hiding. During that time I'm sure my clients thought I'd abandoned them or had been arrested. A lot of my girls went on to work for other agencies, and I can't really blame them. That's just the nature of the business.

CHAPTER 14

Girls I Have Known and Loved ... or Hated ... or Girls Who Have Really Pissed Me Off

You may be surprised to learn that I'm pretty much against prostitution as a concept. I was brought up to know right from wrong. My adoptive parents may have had their problems, but they believed in your basic middle-class values (or, in their case, upper-middle-class values), and they taught them to me before our family fell apart. It's partially because of them that I believe it's important to be straight with people, to treat them how you want to be treated, to approach life's issues rationally instead of flying off the handle and letting your emotions rule you. These qualities, which may seem common enough to most regular people, make me so different from most of the people who work in this business.

You may also be surprised to hear that I do believe marriage is sacred, maybe even more so because of what happened to my parents' relationship. Since almost all my clients are married, I think that what they are doing is completely and totally morally wrong. But I think lots of things we do are wrong, like smoking, for example, and there are lots of people making money off that habit. I try not to judge people because, obviously, who am I to judge?

But truthfully, I can't stand most of the guys who use the service that pays my rent.

Once in a while I'll get a call from somebody's wife, and that's the worst. It usually happens because the wife suspects her husband is cheating on her, so she looks through his phone records or at the numbers she doesn't recognize stored in his cell phone. Sometimes they track me down through credit card statements. Because I have to keep my guard up, stay calm, protect myself and my client, I usually tell a wife: "I'm sorry, honey, but I don't know anyone by that name. I think you must have the wrong number." Although that's what I tell her, what I really want to say is "Yes, your husband's an asshole, and it's worse than you thought. You're probably thinking I'm his girlfriend, but I'm not. I set your husband up with hookers on a regular basis, sometimes as many as one or two a week. Remember when you thought he had to run to the office last Thanksgiving because of an emergency? Well, he lied. He called me. You should really dump him right now. Pack up your stuff and your kids and leave him today. There's no way you need a dog like that in your life."

Of course, I think the clients are worse than the entertainers—they are the ones who have taken marriage vows after all—but the girls are not totally free from blame. They still shouldn't be sleeping with married men. Obviously, they don't always know who is married and who isn't, and that's definitely not a question they should be asking their clients if they're doing their job right. But still, I think they share some of the responsibility. And I do too, for setting it all up.

Now if the guy is single and the girl is single and the girl is doing what she does for the right reasons, then I don't have an issue with taking money for sex. The only problem with that is it usually doesn't happen that way. It usually happens that a girl gets into this business because she's got a nasty drug habit and is desperate for money, or because she's broke (and often a runaway, like Natasha and I were) and desperate for money, or because she hooks up with the wrong guy, who knows how to control her and uses her to make money.

I'd never do what my girls do. It's not so much because I think it's so immoral but more because I just think a person should do more with her life than that. There may not be much wrong with prostitution when it's two consenting adults without risk of collateral damage to wives or kids or whoever, but there's not much to respect about it either. It's like becoming a father: any asshole with a dick can do it, but that doesn't mean they all should.

A lot of my girls accuse me of not having much respect for the women who work for me, and I tell them they're right. That's another reason why I'm not a pimp. I don't bullshit my girls. I tell them in a heartbeat what I really think. In fact, I have more respect for a girl working the street corner than for a girl who works for me, because with a girl on the street, it's just 1–2–3—do your business, give me my money, and get out. And unless she's a junkie or out of her mind, it's done safely, with a condom. In those instances, it's just about sex, but being a GFE escort is about more than that. It's about intimacy or, at least, the illusion of it. The girlfriend experience means the girls kiss, they do oral without. They do use condoms for sex—or, at least, I tell them they're supposed to—but you can still spread things through that level of intimacy. And, obviously, the more intimate you are, the less safe it is for both parties. Honestly, I promote what I think is the worst part of this business because it's the least safe.

I've lost so much respect for women doing this. The truth is, what I do isn't that hard; it just takes some time and discipline to figure it out. If any of the girls who work for me had even half a brain, they'd learn how to market themselves and find their own clients, and then they'd be making a lot more money. But these girls can barely get themselves to work. At least half of them don't even know how to use a computer. It's the nature of the business.

If a girl could do anything else, she probably would. Practically all of them have got something seriously wrong with them—drug habits, shopping habits, boyfriends who treat them like shit. A lot of them are unstable or fucked up in the head. You have to be to do what they do.

Zoe, for example, once went to a salon and got a massage from this really hot guy. The two of them ended up having sex before her appointment was over, and she left him a huge tip for his "services." Then she recommended the guy to a friend who had recently broken up with her boyfriend and needed some action. When the girl approached the masseur about getting more than just a back rub, he was totally offended. "I don't do that," he told her. Zoe's view of the world is so screwed up that she hadn't even realized the guy just liked her and wanted to fuck her. No payment required.

I've truly respected only three girls who've worked for me during the whole time I've been doing this. That's three out of probably hundreds. The first was Angie, who was a college student who worked as an escort to pay her tuition. Unlike most girls, she saved every penny she made, and, boy, was she cheap. She'd wait an hour for my driver to come get her and take her to her hotel rather than take a fifteen-dollar cab. She paid for school that way, and she did other things too, like travel to Europe. She stopped working after a while, and I can only assume she graduated from college and got a better job. She was an entrepreneur at heart, so I'm sure she found something worthwhile to do with herself.

Then there was this girl named Antonia, who still works for me from time to time. She just really enjoys the business and takes it seriously. When clients create their fantasies about the girls they pay for, she's exactly what they think of: some nice, pretty girl who just really loves sex and is uninhibited enough not to feel bad about getting paid for it. Until I met Antonia, I didn't think such a woman existed. (Of course I never tell my clients that. When a guy asks, I just look at him with all the fake sincerity I can manage, and say, "Yeah, baby, they're all nymphomaniacs who just can't get enough . . . every one of them.") Antonia's one in a million, in a billion. She doesn't do it for the wrong reasons. For her this is a life choice. I kind of respect that. Maybe she's hiding some inner demons, but if she is, she has them in check. She's really reliable, and she's a great person.

The third girl was Monique. She had been married, but her husband killed himself. From what she said, he really loved her, he just had problems. He was on medication and had forgotten to take it when he did it. She worked for a while and saved all her money so she could do other things. She was a photographer who came in from Florida to work, but whenever she had spare time she'd go to New York to visit the museums. She also spent half the year in Asia, traveling and taking pictures. She was incredible and really humble too. She showed me some of her work once, and it was really good. She took classes on the side as well. She just did all sorts of things with herself.

Of course, all three of these girls were wildly popular with clients—Angie was the number one earner when she was working—which tells me that they were doing everything and anything. Clients don't rave that much about any girl unless she goes all out, which can obviously be dangerous. I don't know why they were like that. All three of them worked only part-time, so maybe they just wanted to make as much money as they could when they were working. I was always able to book all three of them up with as many appointments as they could handle, and I'm sure they earned some nice tips as well.

Angie, Antonia, and Monique were definitely exceptions to the rule. I also have a good friend who is one of the top porn stars in the country, and she takes home about $10,000 a week working for anywhere from $1,000 to $1,500 an appointment. She doesn't have a lot of repeat business, but she does have a lot of fans who know her from her movies. She has done over a hundred movies to earn that status, however, and she travels about nine months out of the year marketing herself. She's definitely an exception to the rule too, but she's never worked for me because she doesn't need someone like me. Not only does she make tons more money per appointment than my girls but she also pockets all the money herself because she knows how to handle her own business.

Most of the girls in this business are total messes. I even have trouble respecting the ones I've become friends with. For example, my friend Nicole, the one who has kids and is supported well enough by her ex, basically works for party money. That alone isn't so bad, I guess, but not long ago I ended up staying at her house so that I could keep her asshole boyfriend from beating the crap out of her. He was at *her* house, destroying all *her* stuff, and she didn't even throw him out. And it's not like she needs him for anything.

While he went off, Nicole got the hell out of there and hung out at the drugstore for a couple of hours, wandering the aisles looking at toothpaste until her boyfriend calmed down. I went and picked her up there and told her I was on her side. Then I brought her home and told him, "Listen, you can't be doing this to her. She's smaller than you and I'm going to defend her. You know I'll shoot you if I have to." He's a friend of mine too, so he knew that I would.

But then, a couple of days later, it happened all over again. He started beating on her and ran her out of her own house. Again, I went to get her, but this time I told her, "If you keep going back to him, then this is your fault too."

She just looked at me and said, "But if I don't go back, he'll take all my G!" Apparently she had left her stash behind, and that was all she really cared about. I told her how sad and pathetic that was. Then I drove her back home like she asked me to.

Zoe too had a pimp for years before she finally got away from him and came here. He not only took all her money and lived off her (she was his only "employee"), he couldn't even take care of himself. She did all the cooking, all the cleaning, even washed all his clothes. If this guy couldn't even manage a clean shirt by himself, what did she need him for? She told me that since she'd been in New Jersey, one of her friends back home had run into the guy and said he was living on the streets. Without her, he was nothing, and she could never see it.

Zoe has had a self-esteem problem for as long as I've known her. She even worries about what the clients think of her, even the ones who are one-time customers that she'll never see again. She had this one client not long ago who was unbelievable. Even I could barely stand to listen to her tell the story after all I've seen and heard over the years.

We had been traveling as part of the circuit we had set up for ourselves, so we were out of the area where most of our clients live. To see what we could get, I had put up an ad for her on some of the local sites, including Craigslist, which was probably a mistake. Anyone can find you on Craigslist, including the cops, but we figured it was a one-time thing and we could probably get away with it. We got some responses right away and booked a few appointments for her in a different hotel than the one we were staying at so we could at least be somewhat safe. The clients would all be first-timers she didn't know, but she didn't seem to mind. She did that kind of thing all the time when she worked for her pimp in Montreal.

Everything was fine until she got to her last appointment of the day. As soon as she saw the guy, she knew she was going to have a problem. The guy was old—she figured he was at least seventy by the look of him—but he wasn't just old, he was sick. He said he had Parkinson's disease, and she believed him because his hands shook the whole time. And he wasn't just sick, he had hurt himself. He said it was a golfing accident, whatever that is, and he had

187

bandages all along the right side of his body, on his hip and on his ribs. She said you could see the pus and blood oozing through them. When she was telling me about it, I had to stop her right there. That was all the detail I could stand.

When Zoe first opened the door, she wasn't sure what to do with him, so she asked if he'd mind taking a shower. He kind of smelled, and that was *before* he had gotten all his clothes off. But he said he couldn't. He wasn't supposed to get his wounds wet. Doctor's orders. That's when she should have said, "Sorry, I just can't help you."

Just because you're a working girl doesn't mean you don't have the right to set some standards. But Zoe, she's always had a people-pleasing problem. When she told me she had never sent a guy away before for any reason, my jaw nearly hit the floor. "*Why not?*" I asked her. "Because I just don't like doing that to people," she said. Is she afraid she's going to hurt their feelings? I just don't get why she cares.

But that's not my problem. My problem was that when I called Zoe to tell her the hour was up, the guy got upset. He said he needed more time. He hadn't managed to cum yet, which Zoe was thanking her lucky stars about. She said later that if she had seen him cum, she would have lost her lunch right then and there. He threatened to get on the review boards as soon as he got home and write scathing reviews of both Zoe and our agency. He said he was going to let everyone know that we ripped people off and took advantage of a poor old guy.

Since I wasn't there, Zoe had to handle the situation, but I talked her through it. She told the guy that if he was a regular hobbyist who posted often on the review boards, then he should know that if there is one hard-and-fast rule in this business, it's that an hour is an hour, no exceptions. "Most girls would have helped me," he complained. "They would have helped me get out of my clothes and get cleaned up so that it wouldn't take so long."

Zoe wasn't taking that, and I was proud of her for sticking up for herself. "Did it ever occur to you that some people are uncomfortable with all this?" she shot back. "I've been nothing but nice to you and I've tried my best, but I can only do so much!"

You'd think someone like him with all the problems he had would have learned to be a lot nicer to people to get what he wants. I mean, he was in no position to be demanding. He finally did leave, unsatisfied, and I don't think he ever posted a bad review. I never saw one anyway. But even if he had, it wouldn't have been the end of the world. If he had gone through with it, we would have offered a few deals to regular clients in exchange for rave reviews to counter his complaint. If a customer sees one low rating among a whole bunch of perfect tens, he's going to know that that one was a fluke. That guy was definitely not the kind of customer we'd ever want coming back, so fuck him.

It all worked out in the end, but I couldn't believe Zoe had so little self-respect. She should have sent the guy home in the beginning, before things had gotten that far. But she's an equal opportunity ho and proud of it. I just don't think that anyone needs a few hundred bucks that badly. No one needs some G that badly either, but that didn't stop Nicole. She and I were friends until I had to fire her because she had done so much GHB and meth that she defecated in the bathtub of her hotel room and then passed out on the floor, where her next client found her. She left me no choice. All I know is that I don't need anything that badly. And I'm proud of that.

These girls make sick money, disgusting amounts of money, so that's not their problem. The problem with most of them is that they just throw it away so they're never building anything, never working toward anything, never doing anything at all to better themselves or their situations. It's just day-to-day with them. They think they're going to be young forever, but they're not. They can't all be like Nicole and a couple other girls I know who were still working for good money in their forties. Even Nicole probably won't last much longer, not the way she's going anyway. If the girls are lucky enough to live past their prime, then what are their options? End up with some asshole husband who pushes them around? Or maybe work some shitty minimum-wage job at a diner or something? They don't have many options, but they also don't think about alternatives as much as they should.

So do I respect them? Definitely not. Why would I?

Do I feel sorry for them? Sometimes, but not for long. At least I try not to. We all make our own choices, and we are all responsible for our own lives and for what we become.

Epilogue

Sometimes I think that the universe has its own rules and that it has ways of making you follow them whether you want to or not. Things were going pretty well for me until recently. Zoe and I had grown closer and closer. We actually became really good friends. We took care of each other, and I gradually came to trust her enough to make her more than just a supporting player, almost a real partner in my business. We lived together, worked together, traveled together, played together. It was better than any relationship with a guy I've ever had.

But, no matter what I do, life always seems to fall back into the same patterns. It's like the universe doesn't want me to be too happy or too stable for too long. I'm not working at the moment. Will I start up again, maybe somewhere new? I'm not really sure. Things are a bit hot to start working again right away, especially on my old turf, but eventually I'm going to need money. And when that happens, what else am I going to do?

After that call to Zoe's hotel room in Boston, when Officer Dan answered the phone instead of her, I lost track of Zoe. I know she got busted, and I tried to find a lawyer for her, or at least someone who would check on her while she was in jail, but no one wanted to get involved, especially since I had shut down my business and didn't have access to much money. I should have left some stashed somewhere besides our room, like I usually do, but I had gotten sloppy since we were doing so well, and I never got around to it. I know they got her on a weapons charge at the very least. The gun I'd left in the room was unregistered and had been bought illegally. I don't know whether they got her on a prostitution charge too, but I wouldn't be surprised. Either way, she was in the country illegally, so she had to be facing deportation in addition to everything else.

It was just a few months before that we had our own little family going. Then Melissa went back to her mom, Nicole went off the deep end, and now Zoe's gone too. And I'm on my own again.

Sometimes I really want to get out of this business, but as soon as I have that thought, I have another one: What else can I do? I've accomplished plenty in my life, not the least of which is the fact that I'm still alive, which puts me ahead of many of the girls I met and lived with in the various youth hostels, group homes, and state facilities in Maine when I was a teenager. So what's a girl who comes from places like that, a girl with an eighth-grade education, supposed to do? How's a girl who wants to make something of her life and doesn't want to rely on some guy to do it supposed to make it in this world without people walking all over her?

"Get out of the business," you might say. I've had a lot of boyfriends tell me that over the years. But then what? Suppose I swear off the sex business forever. Then what?

My story is obviously not over yet, and I don't know if I will get a happy ending. Or even if I deserve one. Some days I think I have a chance, but others . . . Well, the outlook isn't so good. The one thing I can say is that when I first went out into the world on my own, I was really young. You may think a girl of thirteen doesn't know a thing, but I knew even then that my ultimate goals were going to be respect and success.

I think I have achieved those goals to some degree. Today I am somewhere safe from violence and danger, and that's a long way away from where I started out. That sense of security is something

I created entirely for myself, and even though my life can be difficult and hectic most days, I still seem to find reasons to smile pretty often. I can't ask for more than that, and if there is one thing that I would like girls like me to take from my story, it's this: Be strong and survive. No matter what.

Appendix

So You Want to Be a Call Girl?

THE GIRLFRIEND EXPERIENCE
EMPLOYEE HANDBOOK

Girlfriend Experience was founded in New Jersey in June 2002. Since then, our service has grown to become one of the most reputable and sought-out in all of the Northeast. Our rapid success has been accomplished through honesty, reliability, and exceptional customer service. Here at GFE we value our customers and go the extra mile to show our appreciation by offering them the individual care and attention they deserve. We cater only to an upscale clientele that has been screened to ensure the highest level of safety, and our models are individually selected for beauty, class, and tenderness. Our reputation has brought us to new heights of success; maintaining this reputation demands excellence, patience, hard work, and motivation from everyone involved. Girlfriend Experience would like to open our arms and welcome you to our team.

Appendix

Travel and Accommodations

- Models are responsible for all their own travel arrangements. Before you book your travel, however, your schedule must be approved by GFE.
- Accommodations are provided in reputable, upscale hotels.
- Accommodations can be reserved in advance through GFE once all travel arrangements have been confirmed. Models pay $50 per night for their accommodations when reservations are arranged through us.
- Models can reserve their own hotel accommodations as long as they are in the proper service area and are up to our standards. GFE will pay $50 per night toward the total fee.
- You must arrive on Sunday and check in to the hotel between 3:00 P.M. and 12:00 midnight. Your checkout is Saturday at 12:00 noon.
- Once you arrive at the hotel, you must call and leave a voice mail to let us know that you have arrived and what room you have been assigned.

Preparation

- You may find your work schedule leaves little or no time for meals, so it is important to make sure you have snacks for the week. You may also want to request a mini refrigerator in your room along with a microwave for a quick meal between sessions. All hotels have this service available.
- Request extra sheets and towels from housekeeping. Remember to tip the housekeeping staff and keep them happy.
- Allow yourself enough time to take care of all your personal needs for your entire week before 9:00 A.M. on Monday

morning. You may not have another opportunity to do so during your workweek.

Room Requirements

Your room must be presentable at all times. Presentation is everything! A $100 fine will be issued for each inappropriate room detail.

- Beds must be made or turned down neatly.
- Clothes must be placed in closets and drawers.
- No room service trays should be present at any time.
- TV must be off.
- Hygienic products must be clean and neatly arranged.
- A clean towel must be available.
- Baby wipes, mouthwash, and Dixie cups must be available in bathrooms.
- Soft music should be playing in the background.
- Candles lit. Curtains closed. Mood lighting.
- Smoking is permitted fifteen minutes before an appointment. You must hide all smoking items and use an air freshener immediately after. No smoking during a session.

Personal Presentation

- Proper hygiene is imperative.
- A dress, skirt, lingerie, or silk robe is appropriate attire during a session.
- Hair is to be done at all times.
- Nails must be groomed. No wild or extreme colors.
- Dinner dates and other functions require elegant and appropriate attire.

Proper Etiquette

- Your appearance should be clean and orderly at all times.
- Your attitude should be sweet and pleasant at all times.
- Mind your manners.
- Although this is a business, it should not feel like it for clients.
- Use a kind approach when time is coming to an end.
- Your behavior should show that you are a lady at all times, even under pressure.
- Never discuss the "business" at any time during a session.
- Always make the session feel as though "it is not a service."
- Never rush or make anyone feel rushed. Your time may be limited, but your appearance should never show this.
- Your personal issues should never be discussed or apparent during a session. This is a time for the clients, not a therapy session for you.
- Always be happy, even if it means performing! This is your job.

Personal Touches

Personal touches are important to distinguish yourself from others. Each employee has a style of her own that makes each session more personal and special. The following items are not requirements, only suggestions to make the experience unique and memorable for clients.

- Flower petals on the pillows
- Incense in your favorite scent
- Chocolates on the bedside table

- Beverages on arrival
- Private dances
- Hot oil massages
- Intimate candlelight baths
- Games and toys
- Costumes and role-play
- Sexy movies
- Satin sheets
- Sensual music to set the mood; soft jazz or Norah Jones are excellent choices

Appointments

- Check to make sure the room is in perfect condition before receiving your appointment.
- Be warm, friendly, and courteous at the door—the perfect host.
- Collect funds. You are responsible for the complete fee. If any amount is missing, you are held responsible.
- Offer personal touches and quality time.
- Cuddle and clean up.

Schedules

Reliability is one of our strongest points. Any cancellation within 18 hours before an appointment or failure to receive a client in a timely manner will result in a $200 fine, which must be paid immediately. If contacting you for an appointment becomes difficult, 3 messages will be left on your available number 25 to 30 minutes before your session. We will consider this due notice, and it is your responsibility to receive your session on time.

- Our work hours are Monday thru Friday, 9:00 A.M. to 11:00 P.M. Only repeat clients are permitted to book past nightfall. During these hours you are expected to be available within 30 minutes at all times.
- Your morning schedule is usually given the previous evening to allow you to determine your wake-up call. Leave enough time for your personal needs.
- You should allow yourself enough time in the morning for breakfast before your first session. You may not have another opportunity to eat a meal until the end of your work schedule. This is why preparing with snacks can be very important.
- If you are not given your schedule for the morning, we will notify you with a wake-up call 45 minutes before your first session, 30 minutes before at any other time.
- Schedules change throughout the day, and you must understand that there are many cancellations and last-minute bookings. You must always have your cellular phone open between sessions. If you do not have a cell phone, you are not permitted to leave the room during business hours and must keep at least one hotel line clear for incoming calls.
- Sessions are booked in 15- to 30-minute intervals, depending on what you can handle.
- You are required to work a minimum of 6 hours per day or 30 hours per week.
- You must be ready to receive your clients punctually.
- If your client is delayed, be patient and give us a reminder call 25 minutes after his scheduled time.
- No matter how late a client may be, you must not rush him under any circumstances. Clients are to be given a full hour unless specified by the office personnel.
- If schedules are delayed and sessions run into each other, you must not discuss this situation in front of the clients. Phone

personnel will be waiting for your call to say that you have completed your first session and are preparing for your next. They will not send the next client to you until you have confirmed this by phone.

Finances

- All appointment fees are split, two-thirds to the employee and one-third to GFE.
- All fees from clients are your responsibility to collect. Any loss of income will be paid by you.
- Each day's collections must be placed in a separate envelope. Each envelope will need the following information: name, date, and the total amount in the envelope, as well as a breakdown by appointment (with each client's first initial only!). Monday's envelope should include the total hotel fee for the week.
- All funds should be held in safekeeping and are your responsibility until they can be turned over to management and counted.

Reviews

Reviews are what make GFE one of the greatest services in the Northeast. Each review covers atmosphere, reliability, and most of all, the quality of services rendered. Review boards are used by potential customers to find out more about which ladies they want to spend time with and which ones they want to stay away from. Having all-around great reviews has brought us skyrocketing success in the industry. We would like to maintain these incredible reviews, and through dedication, hard work, and a little direction from us, you will find yourself reviewed as one of the top ladies in the industry.

Photos

Girlfriend Experience would be happy to arrange a photo shoot for you at any time. Photos can be done in 2 ways.

- First, we can share the cost of having photos taken. If we do this, we will retain all copyrights to all the photos. This means the photos can be used only by us, and a lawsuit will result if they are used for any other purpose. If at any time you would like to have the rights back or to use the photos for your own purposes, we would be happy to give up these rights once you have reimbursed us for our portion of the photo fees.
- Second, if the entertainer pays the full amount for her photos, she retains the copyrights to those photos. GFE will use the photos only for advertising purposes. If at any time the entertainer would like her photos to be taken off our advertisements, we will arrange for this to happen within 3 to 5 business days from the request.

Touring

Touring is an important part of GFE. It gives ladies an opportunity to travel and gain new financial opportunities. Touring takes a large amount of time to arrange in addition to the costs of travel and advertisements to make it successful. This is an important commitment. Many clients book weeks in advance for tours, so it is imperative that when an entertainer agrees to tour, she follows through on her commitment.

- A $500 deposit is required for each week you are on the tour. This is a refundable deposit and will be returned when the tour is finished. If the entertainer cancels, the deposit is automatically lost because of the nonrefundable costs of booking a tour.
- All travel will be arranged by the entertainer. If you would like help with travel arrangements, we can get a travel agent to help you for a fee. We will need to be paid in advance for all scheduling.
- It is important to stay on schedule and be on time. All the same rules specified in earlier sections apply when you are on tour.
- You are responsible for all fees owed to GFE. This is very important, so make sure you are especially careful in securing your money and ours.
- Travel dates cannot be changed once agreed upon.

X-treme Rules

Some rules are of the highest importance to the security of our business. Failure to abide by these rules will result in immediate termination!

- Confidentiality is of the utmost importance. There should be no discussion of any kind with anyone about how our business is run or any other details of any kind.
- Clients should never know the number of clients you see, the amount of money you make, or any other details that could jeopardize the safety of our business.
- Your personal information is held in confidentiality. Respect other members of our team and treat them as you wish to be treated.

- We do not allow any exchange of phone numbers or e-mail addresses with clients. If a client hands you a business card, you must decline the offer and return the card to him.
- We do not allow referrals to other businesses by clients or employees. Any discussion of referrals is not acceptable.
- Interacting with hotel guests on a business level is not acceptable.
- Confiding in hotel employees is not acceptable.
- Fighting with a client or GFE personnel, either verbally or physically, is not acceptable.

Some rules are important to ensure that the business runs smoothly and properly and in a consistent manner. Breaking any of these rules results in a $300 fine.

- Any rude or disrespectful behavior toward a client. If a situation arises, call the GFE office immediately without taking matters into your own hands. You will be responsible for returning the client's entire fee to him in addition to being fined if a situation is not handled in the appropriate manner.
- Bad reviews by known reviewers. Reviews are the most important part of our business; they stay with you throughout your career. A bad review can be very damaging to the entire team. The fine is used to pay for the client's next session.
- You must give clients their full time. It is unacceptable to end a session early unless doing so is the wish of the client. Take your time and never watch the clock.
- Your attitude and personal performance is very important. Clients should at no time be made aware of your personal problems. They come to get away from their everyday lives and want to feel no stress. They do not pay to deal with your personal situations.

PIMP AND HO GLOSSARY

Terminology and Abbreviations from the Internet
and the Underground

AKA or Asian   Oral sex on the anus (also called Rimming or
Around-the-World)

Asian Cowgirl   Girl on top, resting on her feet instead of her
knees

Automatic   A girl whose pimp lets her work on her own without
supervision

Bare Back Blow Job (BBBJ)   Oral sex on a man without using a
condom (also called French Without)

Bare Back Blow Job to Completion (BBBJTC)   Oral sex on a
man, without using a condom, to climax

**Bare Back Blow Job to Completion, No Quit, No Spit
(BBBJTCNQNS)**   Oral sex on a man, without using a condom, to climax, followed by swallowing

BBW   Big beautiful woman

Blow Job (BJ)   Oral sex performed on a man

Bottom   A pimp's number one girl or the girl who has been with
him the longest

Break Yourself   Pay your pimp

Choosy Suzy   A girl who jumps from pimp to pimp

Coming Up or Knocking   Stealing a girl from another pimp

Covered Blow Job (CBJ)   Oral sex on a man using a condom (also called French With)

Cowgirl   Girl on top

Daddy   What a girl calls her pimp

Deep   Indicating the number of girls a pimp has working for him, as in "He's two deep" or "three deep"

Deep Throat (DT)   Blow job where the penis is taken all the way into the mouth.

Dining at the Y (DATY)   Cunnilingus

Doggie Style   Man behind girl, standing or kneeling

Dope Boy   Drug dealer

French   Oral sex

Full Body Sensual Massage (FBSM)   Not usually full service, expect only massage and hand job (see definition). Also known as Private Viewing or B2B (Body to Body)

Full Service   Intercourse to completion (with condom!)

GFE   Girlfriend experience. Refers to a type of session that provides a social and physical experience beyond the act itself. More like a date than a quick encounter.

Greek   Anal sex with condom

Greek Without   Anal sex without condom (aka Death Wish)

Half and Half A combination of oral sex and intercourse

Hand Job (HJ) Masturbation by yourself or others

Incall You meet the girl at her place or at a hotel arranged by her

Outcall The girl comes to your place—your home, your hotel, et cetera

Out of Pocket Talking to or looking at another pimp

Porn Star Experience (PSE) A session that feels like being in a porn or XXX movie. Also, a date with a real porn star.

Quota The amount of money a girl is expected to make in order to pay her pimp

Renegade A girl without a pimp

Russian Penis between a girl's breasts until completion

Simp Wannabe pimp

Trap Amount of money made

Turn Out A girl who is new to the pimp and ho game

Tweaker Drug user

Wife-in-Law Another girl with the same pimp

Acknowledgments

First, I want to thank Christa for her amazing strength and ability to piece together the puzzle of my life into something readable. And, while doing so, for being a personal therapist, ally, and dear friend. It has been an amazing experience.

I want to thank Beth Wareham for being a risk taker with a wild streak, which made me comfortable enough to air all my dirty laundry. This book has helped me confront many demons and saved me a ton of money on therapy! Thanks also to Whitney Frick and the rest of the team at Scribner for their support with this book.

I want to thank Carey for being there for me through thick and thin and for never giving up on me even when I would have. It gives me great hope knowing good people do exist in this world.

I want to thank my three favorite hotels for allowing me the pleasure of creating this book from the comfort of my home away from home. (Let me know if you need to collect those smoking fines you always seem to overlook.) Special thanks to Carlos, Martha, Ammira, Evelyn, and Elizabeth; you guys are awesome!

I want to thank my Brooklyn homies who kept me high on life. (Puff Puff Pass!)

And to save the best for last . . . to all my ladies and gents who not only made the survival of a thirteen-year-old runaway possible but allowed me to have a very adventurous, exciting, and fulfilling life that most people could only read about!